THE WINNING SPIRIT

THE
WINNING
SPIRIT

16 TIMELESS PRINCIPLES THAT
DRIVE PERFORMANCE EXCELLENCE

Joe Montana
and Tom Mitchell, Ph.D.

RANDOM HOUSE ⌂ NEW YORK

Published in the United States by Random House, an imprint of The Random House
Publishing Group, a division of Random House, Inc., New York.

RANDOM HOUSE and colophon are registered trademarks of Random House, Inc.

ISBN 1-4000-6444-9

Printed in the United States of America on acid-free paper

www.atrandom.com

2 4 6 8 9 7 5 3 1

First Edition

Book design by Simon M. Sullivan

To Mom and Dad, for all the sacrifices they made.
To Jennifer, who took those sacrifices to the next level.
J.M.

To the winning spirit within all of us.
T.M.

CONTENTS

Introduction

Joe Montana

SINCE RETIRING FROM PROFESSIONAL FOOTBALL A DECADE AGO, I HAVE traveled the country giving speeches on individual and team performance, and attending to my business interests. I am often asked for tips on achieving peak performance, and about winning—in sports, business, and life in general.

I have thought a lot about that word, "winning"—about what it meant to me as a young boy growing up in Pennsylvania, when I probably had a basketball, football, or baseball in my hand 360 days of the year—playing football at Notre Dame and winning a national championship, quarterbacking the San Francisco 49ers to four Super Bowl victories in the 1980s, and later, being elected to the Pro Football Hall of Fame.

My father often told me in my youth that the only way to accomplish anything in sports is to be a winner. Not just to win, but to be a winner. There's a difference. He wasn't constantly telling me to win, win, win at all costs. It was more of a slow teaching process, as we threw the ball back and forth in the backyard, and the lesson was always strive to be the best. To be a winner.

Now, off the field, I still think about winning. Two of my 49ers teammates, Ronnie Lott and Harris Barton, and I started a private equity investment firm when we retired and, with no experience, built it into a growing enterprise with $500 million in assets. We succeeded by knocking on doors that seemed closed—displaying the sort of persistence, discipline, and confidence that we had learned on the playing field. Sure, there were new strategies and rules to learn, but the principles we followed were the same, and we found them surprisingly easy to carry over from sports to business.

The 49ers didn't just win Super Bowls. We possessed an attitude. I call it "the winning spirit," and it was a big part of our success. How do you find the winning spirit? Where does it come from? There is no magic formula. It's about hard work, and it begins with the way each of us prepares for success on a daily basis. However, it is a regimen that can be taught and learned, and it's both self-perpetuating and contagious.

How important is winning?

As I have watched my own children compete in youth sports over the years, I have noticed a growing tendency to deliver pats on the head, to say, "Good job, everyone won today," and to hand out participation ribbons to all who got out of bed and made it to the game. That's not the way I was raised, and I don't dispense that message in my role as a parent. I think it's unfair for a parent to be an uncritical observer of a young person wanting to improve and play at a higher level. As a parent, you need to be not just a cheerleader but a coach. And I believe it is wrong to tell the next generation that they will be congratulated for simply showing up.

Competitive sports are one of the best preparations for life, reflecting, as they do, the highly competitive nature of the world around us. I never wanted anyone on my team, in sports or business, who didn't passionately care about rising above the competition— and winning.

If winning wasn't important, people wouldn't keep score.

Like it or not, we live in a world that keeps score.

Introduction
Tom Mitchell

I AM A PERFORMANCE COACH FOR SPORTS AND BUSINESS CLIENTS, AND my job is to help people perform at their best. I have worked with Olympic, professional, college, high school, and youth athletes, as well as corporate executives and entrepreneurs in a wide range of industries. In both gyms and boardrooms, I rarely meet a person who is not wanting more in life: greater professional success and wealth, personal achievement, or simply health and happiness. Both executives and athletes, I have found, must perform under intense pressure, criticized and evaluated at every turn.

When I began my career as an executive coach, working with business leaders, I found it to be a natural transition in applying many of the same principles I taught as a college basketball coach and sport psychology professor. Both in the world of sports and business, my goal has always been to work closely with individuals, supporting, encouraging, and challenging them to achieve peak performance in their chosen fields.

Over time, I have found myself most interested in coaching individuals who possess a burn—a deep desire to be their best. Although not every athlete will make it to the pros, and not every businessperson will become a CEO, everyone can be the best in his or her own unique way—the best employee possible, the best parent possible, the best friend or colleague.

In the course of my work, I have met some remarkable individuals in business, sports, and the community at large; their stories and the lessons I have learned from them are included in this book. Through the years I've been around many accomplished leaders, and I can say that Joe Montana is one of the best of our time. I am not alone in this assessment. *Sports Illustrated* recently named him the greatest football player of the past fifty years.

The more time I spent with Joe, the more I came to realize how much he embodied the winning spirit. Some of these winning qualities probably came naturally to Joe, but many of them he had to earn through hard work. With the help of his parents, coaches, and teammates, Joe practiced not only drills on the field but inner drills as well. You can see it in the way he communicates, presents himself, and thinks about situations. For example, he has developed a contagious attitude of optimism and trust in achieving what is possible, which leads to confidence in his ability to succeed. I believe this manifested itself in Joe's legendary coolness under fire, when he so often brought his team back from a deficit in the final moments of a game. He expected good things to happen. He expected to win.

Joe Montana understands a wide range of success principles: preparation, attention to detail, enduring setbacks, personal responsibility, honesty, loyalty, and integrity.

Several years ago, Joe and I discussed forming a company to coach and teach time-tested principles that we believe work in family and business environments as well as in sports. We viewed the combination of our efforts as a natural extension of what we were already doing—Joe's speeches and my performance coaching. Together, we could take it to another level. Eventually, Joe and I, along with Hilleary Hoskinson, a marketing, publishing, and technology executive whom I coached for five years, formed MVP Performance Institute (www.MVPperformance.com) to coach and train business executives and others on improving individual, team, and organizational performance.

In *The Winning Spirit,* we lay out our core message, which we have divided into a total of sixteen principles under three general categories. (Joe and I agreed that sixteen was the right number, since he wore number 16 on his 49ers jersey.) Each chapter stands alone and contains a specific message. Take time to let the messages sink in. Together, they are meant as a working guide to show how best to strive for peak performance. The performance principles are easy enough to read and understand, but don't stop there. Those who gain the most will apply them and *practice them.*

My true belief is that the winning spirit exists in everyone. Otherwise, we will have designed a program for only elite human beings born with special gifts, meaning that the rest of us are just ordinary folks with no chance of finding our own greatness. I don't buy that, and neither does Joe.

PART ONE

Individual Preparation

Individual Preparation

INDIVIDUALS PREPARE IN DIFFERENT WAYS. WHAT WORKS FOR ONE PERson doesn't necessarily work for another. Some wait until the last minute. Some require a degree of fear as motivation. Others want to eliminate all distractions, have complete silence, and shut themselves off from the rest of the world. Others prepare with music in the background or in the company of other people. Some need to rehearse over and over until they feel confident. Whatever the method, the goal of good preparation is the same: to ready ourselves for optimal performance, to play or work at our best.

Ideal preparation is more than a physical rehearsal. It should include the mind and heart as well as the body, so that we are prepared on many levels—balanced, centered, and confident.

The six principles set forth in this section reinforce the importance of preparation. We give examples of what works for some individuals, while emphasizing throughout that everyone must find his or her own unique way to prepare.

We do strongly believe and teach that *repetition is king* in the world of preparation. Whether in sports, running the same drills over and over, or in business, practicing a sales pitch or refining a presentation, we gain through repetition a sense of mastery and self-confidence that can be taken into the real game.

Repetition can be a physical endeavor on the court or in the field. It can also be mental repetitions done silently at any place or time. Lying in bed, standing in the shower, sitting in a quiet place, thinking about and rehearsing what we want to make happen. However it is accomplished, repetition is about connecting the mind with the body to achieve peak performance.

While we all tend to rely on preparation techniques we have used successfully for years, we invite each individual to push himself or herself and try some of the different types of preparation in this section.

To be prepared, it's necessary to check in regularly with our individual process and progress. Are we getting enough sleep? Are we eating properly and getting the necessary nutrients? Are we satisfied with our performance? Do we need to make changes? This we know: Excellent performance does not happen on its own. Preparation is required.

We also need to make some personal choices about how we are going to spend our time and energy. How well-rounded do we want to be? Do we want to be an inch wide and a mile deep? Are we ready to put all our effort at excelling in one area, while falling short in others? One thing is certain: It's up to each of us to choose and walk a unique path and, in the process, to design a road map to performance excellence.

Know What You Want

IT'S BEEN SAID THAT CLARITY IS POWER. THAT'S TRUE, BUT CLARITY *put into action* is ultimate power. It is impossible to strive for something until we know what it is we are pursuing. *You have to know what you want.*

Clarity offers a road map as well as the freedom to go after what we most desire. Clarity also provides a built-in filter to reduce the distractions that would interfere with our doing what needs to get done.

To identify what it is we really want requires time and concentration. It can be helpful to write down everything we want to become and accomplish. Even making a simple list may help. We routinely rely on shopping lists; writing down what we want in life can serve as a reminder in the same way.

Getting clear is mandatory. It offers direction and motivation and helps prioritize energy. Whether or not we are conscious of it, most of us want more of something in our lives: more love, more friendship, more meaning, more achievement, more wealth, more health. "More" is seldom achieved without hard work. Having more, or getting more, almost always requires giving more—of yourself.

Not knowing what we want leaves us rudderless in life, unable to muster the direction, drive, discipline, or imagination to *go for it*. To deny or be numb to our wants is to ignore our deepest desires, perhaps to miss out on our truest calling and our greatest joy. Courageously declaring and affirming what we want in life are the best ways to get unstuck—to start generating motion in the direction we wish to head.

Does the importance of knowing what we want seem obvious? If it is so simple, we wonder, then why do so many people stare blankly, become silent, or give a vague response when asked, "What do you really want from life?" and "What is your passion in life?" Asking these questions of ourselves can take more brainpower than some of us are willing to put forth at the end of a hectic day. It may seem too difficult. Or it may seem a luxury rather than an essential act in the course of daily life. To understand our heart's desires takes work, time, and effort. Yet this work is vital for achieving personal satisfaction and professional success.

Questions like "Do I really enjoy what I am doing?" and "What do I do really well?" often have the same answer. Does it come as a surprise that what we like, we are usually pretty good at? And what we are good at, we usually like? Ask yourself. The answers should tell you something important about yourself.

Sometimes the desire for a bigger and better job is actually tied to the desire for one's voice to be heard: more authority, more recognition for our contributions. It is really about designing a great set of questions and answering them honestly.

When we get clear on what we want to achieve, contribute, and possess, our own clarity will guide us like a laser beam directly to the target. We gain confidence through new directions and focus, which convert into enthusiasm, energy, and momentum.

Another gift that comes from clarity is the desire to pursue. When we have a destination, when we see what we want to have, when we feel what we want to experience, a burning passion arises. Clarity unleashes a powerful driving force that is not easily extinguished.

We can all conjure up favorite heroes, in sports or elsewhere. They all have something in common, and in abundance. These heroes are doing exactly what they want to be doing. A long time ago, they had clarity about their chosen fields, and with that clarity came the desire, focus, and energy to practice and excel.

This first principle, knowing what we want, is the beginning of achieving performance excellence. Some may say, "I've already gone through this process, and I know what I want." This is a great place to be. But do not overlook the importance of repetition and review. We should all regularly revisit our goals and dreams, which not only reinforces our desire but also inspires us to keep doing the work that we need to do. Can you imagine a Carnegie Hall pianist saying, "I've already practiced those keys," or an NBA player saying, "I practiced shooting free throws yesterday. Why should I practice them today?" Such statements are inconceivable because true competitors know that repetition is crucial to improvement and success.

Even if we are clear on our goals today, we should expect curves in the road ahead. Ambitions and desires are given to shifts and changes. Perhaps we have pursued something we realize we won't attain, even though we've given it our best shot. Not every college baseball player will play in the big leagues, and not every business major will run a company. Hitting an occasional wall happens in life, so we need to make regular adjustments and additions to our personal "want list."

PRACTICE: Make a wish list of everything you want in life, including both work and personal wishes. Dream big.

Answering a few important questions can be a springboard to finding out what you desire most in life. Ask yourself these questions:

"What do I really want?"

"What are things I want to do, accomplish, and experience?"

Look over your list and choose the one desire that is most important to you at this time. Write down this desire on several three-by-five cards, keeping it simple by using as few words as possible. Put each card in a private place where you'll see it every day, such as a medicine cabinet, a glove box, a wallet, or under a pillow.

Each time you see the card, it will be a reminder of what you really want to achieve and become. It will give you extra motivation and help you stay focused.

This simple exercise will help you become clearer about what you most want. You will soon recognize that the clarity, determination, and drive you are putting forth are bringing you closer to your most cherished goal.

Montana

Recently, after I delivered a speech, someone in the audience asked me how old I was when I won my first Super Bowl.

"Twelve years old, and I've won a thousand of them since." All but four of them, I explained, took place in our backyard in my hometown of Monongahela, Pennsylvania, a few miles down the road from Pittsburgh.

The year I turned twelve, another Pennsylvania boy also won his first Super Bowl. Joe Namath. But Namath wasn't my idol. When my buddy and I played football in my backyard with my mother's clothesline as the out-of-bounds line, I sometimes pretended to be Terry Bradshaw of the Pittsburgh Steelers, even though I never went to a Steelers game. In fact, I never saw a live pro football game until I played in one, ten years later. And yet I kept winning the Super Bowl regularly in my backyard.

My relationship with my dad was all about sports. It was always fun and spontaneous. Sports allowed us to communicate. There was a little shed between our house and the neighbor's. My dad would get his catcher's mitt and lean against the shed, and I'd pitch to him for hours on end. Or we would play basketball, using a hoop that my dad put up over the garage door. We would also go to the nearby basketball court and play one-on-one, or if there was a pickup game going, we would join in. If there wasn't room for my dad in the game, he'd stay and watch, giving me pointers. There was no organized basketball program in town until my dad started one, putting up his own money and running the practices.

My dad got me into organized football at age eight with the local Pop Warner team, which he helped coach. After two years, I was thinking of quitting football and joining the Cub Scouts, like my cousins. I told my dad, and he said it was okay to give up the game if I wanted, but I couldn't quit in midseason. "I don't want you to quit something you've started," he said. By the end of that season, I'd thrown some TD passes and forgotten all about Cub Scouts.

Not long after came that first Super Bowl victory in my backyard. In my heart, I knew early on that sports were what I wanted to do. Though I worked hard at school, I had an intense desire to succeed in sports—and to exceed everyone's expectations.

Mitchell

In coaching people of various ages and occupations, I often work with individuals who are not clear about what they want most in life. Sometimes this lack of clarity can cause an emotional numbness and a state of mental fogginess that is difficult to shake. I hear how a person feels he or she is going through the motions— perhaps earning good money and having the outward trappings of a successful life—but to what end? They feel empty and stuck.

I can say "Know what you want" again and again, but how do people grasp that truth from a numbed state? It is at this point that I like to take them back to their core emotions. Thinking about something is one thing; *feeling* it is an entirely different matter. "What is it you really *love* to do?" I ask.

I've taught junior college athletes who didn't really love the sport they were playing. They may have been naturally athletic, had the right body, or maybe they had huge success in high school. Maybe they were hoping for a scholarship or their coaches and parents were pushing them to play. Regardless, it was not their true passion. Inevitably, that caught up with them, often presenting itself as a kind of cloudiness, a lack of drive and motivation. It didn't make them bad or inept; they were just trying to do something they did not want to do.

Whenever I saw a young athlete struggling in this way, my advice was always the same: "Don't play this game if it isn't what you want with all your heart." It is challenging enough to compete at the collegiate level when you want it and love it, but to do so for other reasons makes the practice regimen a grind and the rewards meaningless.

Outside of sports, many successful people I have known give the same career advice to young people: "Find something you want to do, and success, as well as money, will follow." But what about someone who isn't just starting out and has a family, a mortgage, and other obligations? I have worked with individuals who tell me they would like to change careers but don't know how they will pay the bills. They feel they don't have the luxury to experiment. First I try to find out if they know what they don't like about their current job. Usually, they are surprisingly clear about where they don't want to be. Maybe they have an office job and would rather work outside. Or they have good communication skills but are stuck in a job that doesn't utilize that strength. Or it could be that they don't believe in the product they are selling or the company they are working for. Okay, I say, that's a starting point. One good way to find out what you want is to know what you don't want.

Life is sometimes more about elimination than addition. We eliminate those things that aren't working for us, then see what's left. Now we can begin focusing on those about which we feel more positive.

I don't mean to suggest that tolerance is an unnecessary virtue in life. There are things we do have to tolerate, and we all have occasional bad days at work and at home. The test is whether we are tolerating chronic situations that cause us to be unfulfilled and unhappy. If so, it may be time to draw a line in the sand. "I am not doing that anymore. I don't know quite what it is that I want to do yet, but I know I don't want to keep doing what I'm doing."

Einstein said that imagination is more important than knowledge. If this is true, let's make the time and spend the energy to engage our imaginations and begin to see what it is we want to do

and where we want to go. Let's not allow our own limited thinking (or anyone else's, for that matter) to put us in a box or place a
ceiling above us. Let's utilize the power of clear thinking, as well as
imagination, to help us successfully accomplish our greatest dreams.

Knowing what we want and starting on the path to achieving it
will reward us with boundless energy, hope, confidence, and direction.

Clarity put into action is ultimate power.

PRINCIPLE #2

—————————

Love What You Do

ONCE WE KNOW WHAT WE WANT AND HAVE BEGUN TO PURSUE IT, OUR motivation and passion will begin to flow. If we're driven by our own desire, we feel there is no place we would rather be, nothing else we would rather be doing. Even if we don't relish every single step along the way, our commitment to the goal will carry us through.

To succeed in sports at the higher echelons, athletes must love what they do. It seems absurd to think of a collegiate or professional athlete engaged in a sport that he or she only tolerates. In the course of sports history, it has no doubt happened, probably leading to unhappiness, followed inevitably by underachievement.

We've all heard sports announcers commenting about a particular player "having heart." Seldom are those individuals the biggest or the fastest competitor on the field of play, and the comment is not related to skill level, either. It's about what comes from *inside*— call it heart, call it desire, call it passion. It most often shows itself when an individual is engaged in an activity he or she truly loves. From sports, then, we learn a valuable lesson: Inner commitment, unbridled enthusiasm, and a burning passion to improve are necessary to lift our performances to higher levels.

These traits come from loving something. They come from within us—from a deep impulse all human beings have to find creativity and contentment in doing something for which we ache. Practice or work is no longer an obligation but an opportunity to express ourselves in the moment. Finding pleasure in what we do—in some cases, rediscovering the joy we've lost with the passage of time—is key to happiness and success in any endeavor.

Millions of young men and women play competitive sports, but only a fraction of them will continue on and earn money at the professional level. Yet they all will have tasted the experience of being involved in something they love.

When our sports days (youth or otherwise) are over, is it possible to take that exhilaration into our daily lives? Into the business community? We suggest it is not only possible, it is essential if we want to experience purpose, meaning, and fulfillment in our work. Yet to do so, we must engage in a vocation with the kind of enthusiasm, energy, and mission we felt when we engaged in that sport or activity that brought us so much joy.

How do we find that type of passion for work? What about the reality that we wouldn't be doing this eight-to-five job were it not for a mortgage payment or our children's college tuition?

One may argue that re-creating the joy we found in sports is not always possible—that there is nothing like sports, and we'll never find that kind of pure pleasure in everyday life. Yet the way of the winning spirit is about finding work and avenues of expression that are meaningful. A job, for instance, should be more than simply earning a living, considering how many hours a day and a week we spend on it. It should be a vehicle for pursuing our passion.

When we love what we do, we do it for ourselves, for the enjoyment of the activity, the richness of the relationships, and the feeling of success and well-being that comes from engagement and participation. We do it for all the right reasons. It is not only where we want to be; it is where we must be.

Desire is key to individual preparation. It can't be faked or called up on demand. It comes naturally, from loving what we do. Watch a young child at play. Nothing forced or required; a youngster's energy is boundless and joyful. Desire is the inner energy that gives us the drive to study or practice hard and the passion to excel. Our desire fans the fire that burns deep within, providing the motivation to be outstanding. Desire causes us to lie awake at night, planning what we have to do the next day to succeed. In sports, desire provides the intense motivation and drive to be in the best condition. In business, desire causes us to be creative and hardworking. Desire drives us to discover just how good we can be.

PRACTICE: If you are looking to rekindle the passion and energy you once had, recall a period of time in your life when you were happy and content.

What was happening?

What kind of activities were you involved in?

Who were you spending time with?

Why were you feeling so much joy and satisfaction?

Write down the feelings you had during that time.

Although we cannot live in the past, we can recall the core emotions and attitudes we once experienced, and try to re-create new situations and opportunities that bring forth those same powerful and joyful feelings.

Montana

It's impossible to have the winning spirit without loving and enjoying what we're doing. We won't excel without that intense desire. I'm convinced, after my years of sports, that the only things separating the champions from the also-rans are desire and competitive drive.

When my children tell me they're nervous before a competition or a game, I always tell them that being nervous is good. "The people I don't want on my team," I say, "are those who aren't nervous. That tells me they really don't love what they're doing or care enough to want to perform at their best. An A or an F means the same to them."

I don't want to sound too goal-oriented, but when I was playing in a game, *any* game—Pop Warner, high school, college, or the NFL—the outcome was important to me. Being successful at something we take pride in should be important, although no one is going to win every time. Of course, if we lose too often in sports or business despite our intensity and our drive, we may not be pursuing the right calling.

For me, as soon as the game was over, win or lose, I focused on what I could learn from my actions in this game and take to the next game. I was ready then and there to throw myself into preparing for the next contest or following weekend, because I couldn't imagine doing anything else.

Had I followed my first love, few people would know my name. I wouldn't be coauthoring this book. Had someone asked me when I was in high school what I wanted to do with my life, I would have told them that I wanted to play basketball, my favorite sport. In my junior year at Ringgold High School, we were the Western Pennsylvania basketball champions. I loved running the court, passing to an open teammate, or taking the final shot with the game on the line.

One thing I tell high school athletes is to play the sports they love—all of them. I don't think it's a good idea to force kids to make a choice too early in life. For one thing, they can burn out on a single sport. If I had chosen to play basketball over football, I wouldn't be where I am today. I played the sports I loved and let things work themselves out after that.

In my senior year, I was offered scholarships for basketball and football. I could have played basketball at North Carolina State, which won the national championship that year, and I would have played in the backcourt with the great all-American David Thompson. I went on football recruiting trips to Michigan State, Georgia, Minnesota, Pittsburgh, Penn State, and Notre Dame. My Notre Dame host, a backup quarterback, told me not to go there because it was difficult academically and wasn't much fun: "Go somewhere else and have more fun."

I remained divided between basketball and football, although I knew that as a six-foot-two guy, my chances of playing in the NBA were slim. Riding in the car with my dad one day, I told him I knew what I was going to do. He said he knew, too. He thought I was going to play college basketball. But I had decided on Notre Dame, our favorite college football team, which we had watched together on TV many Saturdays. It turned out to be the right choice.

Later on, if I hadn't enjoyed playing football so much, I might easily have quit in midcareer. It was 1986, and the 49ers opened the season in Florida against Tampa Bay. We won big, and I had a good game, completing thirty-two passes for 356 yards. On one of those passes, I was running to my left and threw back to my right. No one hit me, but as I twisted my body around to release the ball, I felt something snap. I didn't know what it was, and it didn't hurt right away. I stayed in the game.

Only later did I find out I had ruptured a disk and would need surgery. My injury was complicated by a congenital narrowing of the spinal column. None of the doctors seemed certain I would play again, which was scary. My wife, Jennifer, and I were even concerned about my living a normal life, being able to lift and play with our children. After a two-hour surgery, my left foot and part of my leg were numb, a condition that turned out to be permanent. Even so, the doctors saw no reason for it to affect my speed or strength, and they thought I would be able to resume playing with no more risk than I had prior to the injury.

Still, I had a tough time on the road to recovery. A number of times, I came close to shutting it down and calling it a career. I had to learn how to walk again, which in itself was exhausting work. A physical therapist would come to the house every day. Jennifer started getting me moving before the therapist arrived, suggesting that I do some leg exercises to warm up. Between the two of them, I started to make progress.

As my desire and drive returned, I realized this was the only way I could get back to doing what I wanted to do: playing football again. As I progressed from walking to running, it became a contest to see how fast I could be 100 percent again. I needed to get back on the field.

I returned two months after my injury, having missed eight games. We won five of our last seven games that season, and our division. I went on to play eight more years, and we won two more Super Bowls. None of it would have happened if my love for football hadn't rekindled my passion.

When you're doing what you love, it's not about how many points you put on the board one afternoon or how much money you can take to the bank at the end of the week. It's about the pursuit itself. Right now, as a businessman, I want to make a great investment on behalf of my clients, but as soon as I do and get a little charge out of it, I want to find the next great investment.

"Don't they have enough money?" I've heard people say about tycoons like Donald Trump after news of their latest deal. But that misses the point. Even for guys like Trump, it's not just about the money. They love making the deal itself. They want to be involved in the chase and to stay in the game until they close the deal. And once they do—win, lose, or draw—they move on to the next deal with the same intense desire.

It's called playing for the love of the game, and even if they have a few setbacks along the way, they are always successful in the end.

Mitchell

While there is no substitute for hard work when it comes to improving performance, the importance of allowing ourselves to have fun should not be ignored or underestimated.

Making any required regimen feel less like work and more like play—as with the childhood sport we loved so much that we would forget to come in for dinner—leads to improved work habits and heightened skills. I even use this with NBA players who are struggling with their game. I tell them to find that kid they once were on the asphalt playground or in their backyard, to remember the joy and freedom they felt. The results are amazing to see. Still inside every one of us is a kid who wants to come out and play.

Some people believe that it is unhealthy for adults to have too much fun or happiness in life, almost as if happiness were a sin. However, many of the most successful and accomplished people I know are also some of the most playful and happy. I've noticed a tendency among such individuals to appreciate life and possess an attitude of wonder and exploration. They want to share their gifts, to help others find their way, and to make a contribution to the rest of the world. Without their desire for more in life, and the abundances that followed, they would not have been in the position to share. They seem to have let go of the old belief structure that holds it is not okay to have everything you want. These individuals, without exception, have discovered what they love to do, and are doing it.

At the same time, it is unrealistic to think that we will always love our job or that all aspects of work are supposed to be enjoyable and meaningful. However, even while engaged in tasks that are not enjoyable, replacing an "I have to do this" attitude with "I want to do this because . . ." will show positive results, as it did for Joe when he was in rehabilitation after back surgery.

Several years ago, I worked with a senior corporate executive who had lost the feeling of purpose and joy in his life. He held an important position, knew his job was making a contribution in the world, had a good family, and made excellent money. What's wrong here? you might ask. He felt unfulfilled, and in spite of his outward successes, he was struggling to find a sense of personal satisfaction.

After discussing with the unhappy executive what a purposeful life would feel like for him, I began to suspect that it wasn't his job or career that needed changing, but rather, a shifting of his priorities in life. (Again, clarity is essential preparation, because you have to know what you're striving for before you can set off in pursuit of it.) I specifically asked, "What does it feel like to have satisfaction and joy in your life?"

It turned out the executive didn't feel good about the limited amount of time he spent with his family, and how quickly his children seemed to be growing up without him. Preoccupied with work day and night, and on weekends and vacations, he felt terribly out of balance. The signals for him were everywhere: He no longer found fulfillment in his work, he couldn't enjoy his external success, he had seemingly lost touch with his wife, whom he still loved, all of which left him with a core emptiness.

A juggling act of the type this executive performed is never easy—few of us will find any formula to be permanently successful. Rather, it has to be an ongoing process. The truth was that the executive did have major responsibilities outside the home, and he couldn't be in two places at once. But we came up with a strategy, some changes small, others larger. For example, setting aside time during the day—at work and at home—when he would engage in only one activity and not multitask, pouring all his focus, mind, and heart into that activity or person. Also, putting key dates for his children (soccer games, dance classes, etc.) on his schedule at work, thereby assigning them as much importance as any other calendar items, as well as allotting time for him to attend; limiting himself to an hour a day on his cell phone while on vacation. These new behaviors were not as easy to implement as one may think. But in time, these changes began creating positive results in his life. Within six months, he had renewed his vitality for work, and most important, his relationship with his wife and children greatly improved.

Once we have identified the adjustments to our lives that will give us more satisfaction, the real work starts. The trick—and it can be learned—is to begin creating those feelings right away, starting today, and then use them as a road map to move surely in their direction.

As an analogy, I suggest the example of a singer performing a cappella. She is creating tones, pitches, and sounds from her belly, chest, and throat without the accompaniment of an orchestra. Beautiful music is created only from what is inside the singer. We need to do the same thing in creating the feelings of joy, purpose, satisfaction, and yes, love. We want to be able to create those feelings out of thin air, alone, and regardless of our surroundings.

All of us have found ourselves at times without much external support. Maybe we're on a bad team, or our peers at the office are unhelpful, or other issues are working against us. Those are the times to see how much energy and emotion we can muster from within, those feelings of joy and purpose that we can summon from inside like the singer bringing forth music. Once we are able to do that, we may find that little in our external world needs changing. But if drastic change is necessary, then we can go out into the world and do what's necessary to redirect our life—find a new job, set goals, and achieve results—with the knowledge that we control our feelings without depending on others and in spite of our situation.

We should have a real burn inside if we wish to continually take our game to the next level—to achieve excellence because we love what we are doing and because it feels good doing it.

Love that burn, and keep loving it.

Practice with a Purpose

EVERYONE WHO HAS BEEN SUCCESSFUL IN HIS OR HER CHOSEN FIELD understands the importance of practice and preparation. To become outstanding in a particular area, we must learn to practice with concentration and focus. Practice is our chance to work on weaknesses and get better. When we're working to excel in something, it is not enough to do what is expected. We must constantly strive to exceed our own expectations. Nor should we keep starting and stopping a practice regimen. When we practice, we need to be consistent.

What would a great practice look like for you? When preparing for anything meaningful in your life, what would be the most effective use of your time? In what ways can you put forth extra effort and exceed expectations? For a swimmer, it might mean lowering her time for each stroke set by increasing her effort; a golfer could aim to make as many putts in a row as he can from five feet; a basketball player may stay after a grueling team workout to make a hundred three-point shots; an ice-skater might do two extra-clean programs for an upcoming competition. An executive who has to give a presentation could practice in front of a mirror or into a tape recorder or video camera until it's just right—not once or twice but three times or more—making a point to work on smoothly addressing the toughest questions from a harsh critic.

Practice time is an opportunity to improve our game, whatever that game may be. There are a multitude of skills to develop and fundamentals to work on. We train ourselves to put everything we've got into our practice sessions. If there is a secret to making the most out of each practice, it is this: *Enjoy the drills that improve your skills.*

If someone in a leadership role is responsible for conducting practice sessions or meetings, that person's enthusiasm will cascade down to the people he or she is leading. A retired soccer coach used to conduct practice on a field that had no grass, just dirt. It was often hot and windy, and the dust made it difficult to see and breathe. The kids she coached were from a lower-income side of town, but despite a lack of grass, or money for the best equipment, the team went on to be very successful. When asked how she kept her players motivated under such adverse conditions, the coach replied that she enjoyed the practice sessions so much that the kids started loving practice as well.

The most successful athletes consider practice as a privilege and an opportunity. It is also a finite period of time in the day. It has a beginning and an end. Even in the NBA, where players are paid millions of dollars a year to excel, team practice sessions usually last no longer than two hours. There is really no excuse not to "bring it" to each and every practice.

In planning a practice, there are usually many skills to work on. How can you maximize the time?

For starters, avoid trying to work on too many areas in one session. Concentrate on the most essential skills needed for an upcoming event, performance, or game. One week a basketball team might emphasize defense, such as employing a full-court press. The next week a new offensive set could be the main focus.

This variety applies to non-sports fields, too, where adding a new mix of activities can help avoid the feeling of drudgery. One innovative business executive creates a new theme every quarter for his employees to focus on, such as "Seek to Understand" and "Be Quick but Don't Hurry." Through e-mails, posters, and other notices around the office, he gets everyone thinking about how to improve in one specific area, while giving them a beginning and an end, which helps to keep everyone fresh. He has found that it raises efficiency as well as fostering spirit inside his organization.

Practicing with focus, intensity, and enjoyment is part of the equation; practicing intelligently and creatively is equally important.

Another area of personal preparation to be mindful of is having the needed energy to be at our best. If you are not feeling healthy, full of vitality and enthusiasm, you may not have the endurance to lead or contribute to your company, your team, or your family. This kind of preparation entails finding a personal balance in exercise, rest, and nutrition, all of which play vital roles in the quality of a performance in any field. It is important to find and maintain a balance in life—physical, mental, and spiritual—so that we will have the health, vitality, and energy needed to excel.

There may be times when the routine of practice gets old. Perhaps the challenges of daily life intrude and we feel overwhelmed. We may lose some of our energy and competitive edge and feel like we need a break. This is natural. The truth is that a break is occasionally necessary to recharge and renew motivation. Sometimes we might need to take time off to recharge our bodies and minds.

PRACTICE #1: When preparing for anything, try to eliminate the words "I have to" from your vocabulary. Replace such thinking with "I want to." The words "I have to" come up often in our daily lives, but they have nothing to do with following our heart's desire. When we follow our passion, practicing and putting in extra time, affirm things we want to do, not things we have to do. Make this your mantra: "I want to practice. I want to work hard to improve. I'm here because it's something I love to do."

PRACTICE #2: It is a good practice to keep a performance journal. Doing so will help you keep a record of your progress and allow you to become clearer about what you want to accomplish. You may find that writing down your thoughts and feelings increases your motivation and confidence. Writing often makes things more "real." Your desire and emotion can come through, and the power of your own words can inspire you. Keep your journal in a place where you will use it regularly. Write down your hopes and dreams, your successes and achievements, your fears and failures. Whenever a new goal or dream pops into your head, write it in your journal. If your performance is worth doing and your goals are worth accomplishing, they are worth recording.

Montana

My first serious practice sessions were with my dad, who worked with me on perfecting my passing arm and accuracy. A neighbor had a tire swing in his backyard, and my dad had me throwing the football through the tire as he swung it back and forth.

One winter I found a more interesting way to work on my accuracy. From a neighbor's yard, I threw snowballs at the passenger windows of passing cars, then ducked out of sight. It went well until someone called the police, and I got a ride home in a patrol car. Although I explained to my dad what a great drill it was to improve my accuracy, he was not persuaded.

Years later, as a guest on *The Late Show with David Letterman,* I was taken to the sidewalk in front of the theater for an on-camera stunt that had been arranged. Three New York taxis were lined up, and one by one, as they drove by, I was to try and throw a football through the open passenger window. "I want to tell you, Joe," Letterman said, "there were two guys here before you who didn't make one. You might know them. Aikman and Young." The competitive juices began to flow. When the first taxi went by, I hit the post between the front and back windows, and the ball careened away. As the second taxi passed, I lofted the ball through the open window and nearly beaned the cabbie. Game over. The first person I called when I got off the show was my dad. "I told you that snowball-throwing drill would come in handy someday," I said.

Whenever an aspiring young athlete asks for my advice, I say one word: "Practice." Then I add, "There's no shortcut to athletic success." It always comes down to preparation. I never felt I could be in too good a shape or too prepared. I never felt I was accurate enough with my passes. I could never study enough game film or go over my playbook too much or study too hard. Whenever I walked off the practice field, my goal was to be a better player than when I arrived.

When I joined the 49ers, I learned a whole new way to practice and prepare from head coach Bill Walsh. He always pushed us to learn new things. Some weeks he would install thirty or more new plays, and the offense had to learn them against several different defenses. Those were just the new ones. Each week we would have eighty or ninety passing plays in the game plan, with two or three formations for each one. And another thirty running plays. Most pro teams would go into a game with maybe thirty passing and fifteen running plays.

Practice days were long, starting at eight-thirty A.M. with a quarterbacks' meeting that lasted about four hours, during which we watched film of our next opponent's defensive formations. After a short lunch, practice started at one-thirty P.M. and lasted for two hours. Then there was another meeting until five P.M. Most nights at home, after dinner, I was hitting the books, going over the plays, and looking at more film I had brought home.

After each Sunday's game, I had to erase all those plays from my mind and start over on a collection of new plays for our next opponent.

For each passing play, I had to memorize the routes that five receivers would be running—square-out, hook, etc. They were prioritized by who I would look for to throw the ball to first, and if he was covered, who came next. In Coach Walsh's offensive scheme, it wasn't uncommon to check off two or three receivers and be throwing to the fourth or fifth option. The receivers knew that, too, and had to stay alert and be ready for the ball at all times.

With Coach Walsh's West Coast offense, as it came to be known, we wanted to apply constant pressure to the defense. The more pressure we applied, he preached, the more success we would have. We tended to go after certain parts of the field: the left and right "flats" ten to fifteen yards off the line of scrimmage;

medium right and left, some ten to twenty yards deeper; and the area underneath the linebackers, which often presented a nice seam in the defense to attack.

Coach Walsh had us practice and train for the unexpected and the worst situations—just like my dad had taught me years earlier. Coach Walsh would have me call an audible for a running play against a defense designed to stop a run, not something I would usually do in a game. Our defense knew all our audibles, so they knew exactly what was coming their way. These plays hardly ever worked in practice, but when we called them in a game—against an unsuspecting defense—they would often succeed.

At one Pro Bowl game, Coach Walsh was the coach for the National League, and Joe Theismann of the Washington Redskins was one of our quarterbacks. When we first met early in the week to go over the game plan, Coach Walsh handed out thirty passing plays. Theismann came up to me afterward and said, "This is awesome. I can't believe he gave us all the passes on day one."

I laughed. "Bill will keep installing plays until Saturday." He thought I was joking, but I wasn't.

Sure enough, by the end of the week, Coach Walsh had handed out about fifty more passing plays—eighty in all. It was tougher on Theismann and the rest of the team than on me, because I already knew most of them by memory.

Even the experts need to study and learn each week. In fact, the experts who don't study will soon no longer be the experts. They will be replaced by others who work and study harder.

Coach Walsh had us practice things that seemed nuts at the time. Goofy plays. A lot of people remember "The Catch," which led to our defeating the Dallas Cowboys and going to the 1982 Super Bowl, which we won. I threw a very high pass to Dwight Clark in the back of the end zone—it was that high because I was rushed and went down after I threw it. He went way up for it and held on. I really didn't know just how high I'd thrown it until I saw the replay in the locker room. The funny thing was—and most people don't know this—Dwight and I had *practiced* for the possibility of my being rushed and having to throw it that high and his having to go way up in the air to make the catch.

A classic example of practicing with a purpose happened in the 49ers training camp during the summer of 1985. We had all been hearing about a rookie who had been drafted sixteenth in the first round by the 49ers. We were told that, in college, he threw for touchdowns, caught touchdowns, and ran for touchdowns. The kid was supposed to have great hands, but none of us had seen him play, as he had gone to a small college in the Deep South, Mississippi Valley State. The first day of practice, I threw him passes, and he kept dropping them. It was kind of embarrassing as the ball bounced off him and slipped through his hands. Oh, no, I thought, another wasted draft pick.

But finally, he caught his first pass. Normally, in practice a receiver would run about ten yards after catching a pass, jog back, throw the ball in, and wait in line to do the drill again. Not this kid. The rookie tucked the ball away, turned upfield, and sprinted full-speed to the goal line sixty yards away. He caught the next pass, and sure enough did the same thing, and the next one, too. Whatever the drill or pattern—whether the end zone was ten yards or ninety yards away—it didn't matter. Every time he caught the ball, he sprinted for a touchdown. It got to be ridiculous, because we had to wait for him to come back to run another play. The veterans laughed, joked, and razzed the kid for such obvious rookie behavior. His name? *Jerry Rice.*

Does anyone believe it's a coincidence that today Jerry Rice is the number one touchdown reception leader in the NFL, considered by many to be the greatest receiver ever? Of course not. That's the way he practiced every single day.

Jerry continued to struggle that first year, however, and started only four games. He kept dropping passes in games and even heard boos from the home crowd. At times he appeared discouraged.

The coaches told him, "Just keep working hard." Jerry did, and in his breakout game on a Monday night against the L.A. Rams, he caught ten passes for 241 yards and set a new team receiving record. He ended the season strong and won league Rookie of the Year honors. He was on his way to a great career.

The play I remember best from that night against the Rams—and one that revealed the kind of stuff Jerry Rice was made of—wasn't even a pass he caught. We were back deep in our own territory, and I threw a pass from the four-yard line to another receiver, John Taylor, who ran ninety-six yards for a touchdown. But John wouldn't have scored if Jerry hadn't thrown a block twenty yards from the other team's end zone. If Jerry hadn't prepared and practiced the way he did, he wouldn't have been eighty yards downfield to make that block.

The way we practice, and the work ethic that we bring to that preparation, may not be obvious right away, but eventually, it will show.

Mitchell

A couple of years ago, I was hired by a CEO of a medium-size company to help him work on his team dynamics. One of the first things we did was conduct a 360-degree feedback process in which he received positive and constructive feedback from the executives and managers who reported to him. Lots of constructive information came from these assessments. While he was considered an effective leader, there was one glaring area: Many felt he was too distant and removed, especially toward them personally. After we discussed the results, the CEO said he wanted to improve himself in this regard.

We set up a regular time each week—two hours every Tuesday—for him to interface one-on-one or in a small group with his em-

ployees at various levels. The plan was for him to practice asking
meaningful questions and listening to the answers. He became
genuinely engaged in this practice and open to the suggestions and
needs of his employees.

Had the CEO started this practice and stopped, it would have
sent a terrible message—worse than if he had never begun the sessions. But he stuck with it, and he ended up far exceeding the results he sought. A feedback session six months later revealed that
he had gained a reputation as a leader who took the time to listen.
He learned that people did not want to know how much he knew
until he showed them how much he cared.

Practicing with a purpose is also about practicing with efficiency. Sometimes less is more. When I was a college basketball
coach, I scheduled practice sessions that ran for two and a half
hours. Some of my players felt those practices were too long, and
they asked me to shorten them. I thought about it and decided to
make them a deal. If we could get as much done in a shorter practice as a longer one, I would agree. That meant they had to bring
more energy and intensity to our practices. They uniformly did so,
and as their motivation and desire increased, our won-loss record
improved.

When it comes to practicing with a purpose in sports, I think of
Chris Mullin, a six-foot-seven forward out of St. John's University
who won two Olympic gold medals (in 1984 as a college player
and again in 1992 as a pro) and the John R. Wooden Award as the
best college basketball player in 1985. He had a sixteen-year career
in the NBA. He established himself as a hustling, versatile player at
both ends of the court, and one of the great pure shooters in the
game, averaging 18.2 points per game. None of it came easy for
Mullin, who faced some tough challenges on and off the court.

Although Mullin found early success in the NBA, by his third
year in the league, he was overweight, unhappy, and struggling.
Midseason in 1988, he sought help for alcohol abuse, spending a

month in a residential treatment facility. He came out a changed man; he had become clear about what he believed in and the things he stood for. The following season he rededicated himself to the game and averaged more than twenty-five points per game for the next five consecutive years.

A highlight of his career was being selected as a member of the 1992 original Dream Team with the likes of Magic Johnson, Larry Bird, Michael Jordan, Charles Barkley, Patrick Ewing, and Karl Malone. "Sometimes I would ask myself," Mully told me, "how was it that I was able to earn a spot on the best basketball team ever assembled?"

The ultimate gym rat, Mullin spent countless hours honing his shooting touch and conditioning his body. Methodical preparation and practice were keys to his athletic success. His love of the game—playing with his brothers for hours on end when he was young, and sneaking into the gym at midnight to practice his shooting—made the work and practice a joy for Mullin, because there was nothing he would rather be doing.

In 1996, I traveled with Mullin's team, the Golden State Warriors, on some road games as a team consultant. We were in Los Angeles to play the Lakers, and after the traditional shootaround on game day at the home team's court, everyone was leaving to board the team bus. Mullin said he wanted to stay and would take a cab back to the hotel later. He asked me to stay and rebound for him. I was in dress clothes and leather-soled shoes, which never should have been allowed on the court, since they scuffed up the floor, but Mullin didn't seem to mind. He said he wanted to shoot a hundred three-pointers before we went back to the hotel. He began in one corner, where he shot ten, then slid to another spot and shot ten. In all, he stopped at ten places in an arc twenty-four feet from the basket, taking ten shots from each one. He made ninety-six out of a hundred, with me feeding him and counting.

There was only one other person in the gym, and he turned out to be a technician for ESPN. He had been sitting a few rows up behind the basket. He came up to me afterward and said in awe, "I have not seen a shooting display like that since I covered Larry Bird at the Boston Garden."

Many times after that I rebounded for Mullin, whose daily routine often included a hundred three-point attempts. Although I never saw him make ninety-six out of a hundred again, he regularly hit between eighty-five and ninety. Once I counted fifty-seven makes in a row from the three-point line.

There have been many other great shooters in the game of basketball, but I am not sure there were ever any with the same accuracy, consistency, and ability to remain focused under fatigue that Mullin possessed. Through the years, I have asked Mullin about the art of shooting a basketball, and he will give a few pointers having to do with technique, focus, and where to look on the rim. Inevitably, he always comes back to the same words: *repetition, repetition, repetition.* The best way to become an excellent shooter is by practicing shooting the basketball.

Putting in the extra time works in other areas, too.

Strive for Excellence

STRIVING FOR EXCELLENCE IS AN ESSENTIAL INGREDIENT IN DEVELOP-ing the winning spirit. Achieving excellence is about surpassing expectations—our own and those that others have for us—and reaching for new heights. To achieve these heights requires hard work, for which there is no substitute.

Being excellent does not always come naturally. It is often a learned skill. Effort is required—at times huge, concentrated effort. The hard work is not just physical effort but mental effort as well. Staying mentally focused on our ultimate goal is as important as any physical regimen.

We attract to ourselves what we focus on. Our power to set a course of action should be part of every workout schedule and every business plan. If we concentrate intently on excellence and success, eventually we will find excellence and success. If we contemplate the possible and look for opportunities everywhere, the world becomes a place filled with possibilities and opportunities. If we think we are strong and capable of heroic deeds, one day we will be.

PRACTICE: Spend some time observing the work ethic of people you work with or compete against. Study their habits, their attitudes, and their eagerness to get in there and get the job done. See if you can find people who don't make excuses, who put in extra time and effort. Look for those who can give and take constructive feedback, who bring out the best in others. After several weeks of observation, write down the names of three people you found who prepare, practice, and work with real effort. Then ask yourself if you would be on their list if they were doing the same exercise. If not, what would you need to change or do to make someone's list?

Montana

Whether at practice or during a game, whenever I stepped onto the field, I always tried to complete 100 percent of my passes. I obviously never did, but that didn't keep me from trying each and every time.

I always remembered my dad's advice from when I was growing up and learning new activities: "Whatever you do, Joe, you should want to be the best." It sounded pretty good to me, but it was some years until I learned all that would entail.

When I joined the 49ers, Bill Walsh made it clear that he expected all of us to strive for perfection. That was his standard of excellence. It started with everyone being on time, and it spread to the practice field, where he wanted everyone to work hard and smart every day.

I had been playing football for ten years and had just won a national championship at Notre Dame when I showed up on the 49ers practice field in Redwood City, California, that first summer. Coach Walsh took me straight back to the fundamentals of playing quarterback. Basic footwork, throwing position, and understanding of the game. It was somewhat surprising at first, because I thought I was past all that. Coach Walsh explained to me that first day that his style of football was built around quarterback fundamentals. Everything was about timing.

I worked on my drop-backs after the ball is hiked—three-step, five-step, and seven-step drops. If I didn't do them correctly, Coach Walsh said, whatever else I tried wouldn't be right, either. If my offensive linemen thought I was taking seven steps, they knew how far they could step back and how long to hold their pass blocks. But if I took only three steps back, they and the defensive guys trying to sack me would be in my face before I knew it.

Coach Walsh was a stickler for details. He had me practice throwing the ball on a crossing route not eighteen inches in front of the receiver, or six inches behind, but exactly twelve inches in front of the numbers every time. That way the receiver could concentrate on catching the ball and not worry about the defender bearing down on him at full speed.

I had been throwing hook patterns for half of my life, but Coach Walsh taught me something new. When the receiver curled back toward me, I should aim for the number on his jersey that was on the opposite side of the direction the defender was approaching from behind. That way the receiver knew which way to turn after the catch to avoid the defender. For example, if the defender behind Jerry Rice, who wore number 80, was approaching from Jerry's left, I would aim for the number 8. That signaled to Jerry that he should turn to that side—his right—after making the catch. Practicing the smallest details every day can be tedious, but they will pay dividends.

As I look back, I realize that I learned about performance excellence from a master. Coach Walsh kept hammering home that we had to strive for perfection even though none of us was perfect. At times we would fall short, of course. But if we were going for perfection, Coach Walsh figured that even with mistakes, we could still end up being the best on most Sundays. He was correct.

I think about those lessons today. Whenever I walk into an important business meeting, I still want to complete 100 percent of my passes—only now I hope to get 100 percent of the deals I'm looking for. That rarely happens. Things change in the course of negotiations—you realize this part isn't going to work, or something new comes up that needs to be considered. So we start making adjustments while keeping our end goals in mind and never settling for "good enough." Being prepared for the unexpected and making the necessary adjustments are what performance excellence is all about.

Football is a feedback-rich environment. You are told what you did wrong every time you leave the field. You have to learn from that feedback rather than taking it personally, a lesson that people in other professions could learn from. It's not always easy to listen to criticism, but it is important to be open to improvement, if reaching a level of peak performance is your goal.

I have never liked losing. In fact, I have hated it for as long as I can remember. Growing up, I had this neighbor who was a few years older. He wasn't a great athlete, but he was a tough kid with a big heart who didn't like to lose. And whenever he beat you at something, he'd never let you live it down. So I grew up working hard to try to beat him every time.

Winning only a certain amount of the time has never worked for me. I still remember the last game of the regular season one year. We had already won enough games to get into the play-offs. We should have won but had a letdown and lost. As a result, we had to go back to Buffalo for the first-round play-off game. We had beaten Buffalo earlier in the year, but it was a nasty day—30 degrees, with the wind howling and a freezing drizzle. The ball was constantly slippery, and I couldn't throw it over fifteen yards. We lost. End of season. If we had won that last regular-season game, we would have been playing that day in Kansas City, where it was 50 degrees, with the sun shining.

In business, if you don't make a quota for the month, you may not make your quota for the year. That could mean you don't get your bonus, and you may fall from being the top salesman to number two, which for me has always been first place for the first loser. I'd rather be the first winner.

Mitchell

Shortly after I graduated from college, I spent some time with a group of Trappist monks who had devoted their lives to the search for God. Were any of them without imperfections and weaknesses? We all have so many temptations, and can trip up in so many ways, yet these individuals had given their lives to trying to attain a kind of spiritual perfection. I didn't think for a second that any of them would ever find that perfection, in this world at least, any more than the rest of us would, but they were inspiring, regardless. I understood that the journey they were on—the way they had chosen to live—was the vital part.

I coached an executive for more than a decade and have seen him in different positions as he worked his way up to CEO. From the beginning, I could see that he set out to excel in every one of his jobs. It's easy to say, "I want to be the best," but to walk the talk, lots of little things come into play. I studied his behavior—learned how he got up in the morning with self-administered pep talks, how he communicated with his employees by asking questions and listening well, how he delegated not by simply issuing orders but by giving employees a real say in something they knew about. I watched him empower his employees and thereby have them feel ownership and responsibility in their jobs. He clearly expected excellence of himself and others as well. He knew how to defuse tension and unnecessary pressure in those around him by acknowledging their victories, no matter how large or small. He successfully managed not only from the top down but from the bottom up by including trusted employees in major decisions. I could see why he was someone other people wanted to perform their best for. The most valuable lesson I gained from him was to watch him call forth an inner power—a driving, steadfast will—for achieving excellence. I watched him command maximum effort from himself, which would naturally cascade down to others in his orbit. He would constantly say, "Create your own success today. Don't wait for it to come to you."

When it comes to creating excellence in any field, wealth and station in life are no assurance of achievement. Often we see, in sports and life, that the child who has everything handed to him or her doesn't possess the inner fire to strive for greatness. On the other hand, we find, regardless of lack of parental support, lack of funds, even lack of education, a desire to better oneself can overcome these and other formidable obstacles. In fact, some of the most determined and successful people I know have come from backgrounds of incredible hardship. Several professional athletes I have worked with talk about how their desire to pull both themselves and their families out of poverty fueled their competitive spirit.

At the same time, the competitive spirit can and should be fun. I coached a business executive who told me about one of his top salesmen, once a wrestler in college. He loved all forms of competition, looked for the game in everything, and, in the process, honed his skills. Every week was a new competition for him, starting on Sunday, when the company released its weekly numbers. Every Sunday morning, he would put his wife and baby on a city bus at Fourteenth Street in Manhattan, and he'd take off running. His goal was to beat the bus to Fiftieth Street—for a while, he was even more motivated, because his wife was pregnant with their second child, and it was difficult for her to get off the bus with their toddler without assistance. If he was late, she was unhappy. After the bus run, the salesman, still sweaty, would go to the office, turn on his "lucky" computer—the same one where he looked up the results every week—and see if he had beaten the previous week's number. At that moment, he immediately began to focus on how he could do better the upcoming week. His Sunday run and visit to the computer to get his numbers were a weekly goal that gave him a clear incentive to drive hard into the new week. It was a game, but it was also about competition and getting business done. Not surprisingly, this hard charger moved steadily up the ranks and became a leading executive.

Although we may not all want to be as extreme as the bus-racing salesman, each of us should look at life and find at least one area where we really want to push ourselves to be the very best—as a parent, a student, an employee, an athlete—where we can strive for excellence and discover just how good at something we can become.

Find the Confidence Within

ACQUIRING CONFIDENCE IS A BUILDING PROCESS THAT WE MUST LEARN and practice like any other skill or technique. Although we may be born with certain inherent gifts, developing our confidence will help us bring out these natural talents.

Confidence is trusting in our abilities, a feeling that our best effort will result in our intended goal. Success and confidence are symbiotic: The more we have of one, the more we find of the other. The greater our trust in ourselves, the greater our ability to inspire others—coworkers, teammates, family members, friends.

While some fortunate people get much support and encouragement from others, less fortunate ones have to manage on their own. Either way, self-esteem, a vital component of confidence, is a prerequisite for a successful and happy life. You must believe that you are worth it. You must know that out of everything you do, you are your most important project.

Building confidence and self-esteem often involves making changes in our lives, which takes practice. Often a good way to get started in building confidence is to increase our physical energy level. By taking excellent care of our bodies—eating a nutritious diet, getting regular exercise, sleeping enough, meditating, nap-

ping, and developing other self-nurturing practices—we will recharge and revitalize ourselves, which makes it all that much easier
to succeed.

To gain confidence, you must break old habits that have been
limiting and unproductive, then develop new, more positive ones
in their place. Eliminating the habit of negative thinking is crucial.
Some of these thoughts have been embedded in our mind for so
long that we assume they are permanent—and worse, we believe
they are true. Neither is the case. We should avoid telling ourselves
negative things. There will be enough negativity coming our way
from the world around us. Why let it come from within, too? Si-
lencing the inner critic that tears us down is crucial to building
confidence.

Making encouraging statements to ourselves also builds confidence. These statements—sometimes called "affirmations"—are
inspirational words or phrases that we repeat to ourselves to help
remember what it is we want. An affirmation should be positive,
easy to say, and worded as if its goal has already been achieved. Affirmations are like tiny seeds planted in our minds, and with practice, the ideas start to take root in both the mind and body,
strengthening our self-confidence.

One of the top college swimmers on the West Coast—a consistently fierce competitor—uses an internal pep talk before a big
meet. For her, it takes the form of: "I am ready. I am prepared. I
deserve this moment." A professional golfer uses a one-word affirmation before teeing off: "Home." It is the most relaxing and cen-
tering thing he can think of when addressing the ball.

Once we've stopped judging ourselves so harshly, we also need
to avoid blaming other people for what has happened to us. As we
learn to forgive ourselves for past mistakes, we must also learn how
to forgive others. Keeping grudges takes up much more energy
than reaching reconciliation.

Recognizing our hidden fears and bringing them into the light
is another way to increase our level of confidence. Upon examina-

tion, our fears are often exposed as groundless, yet they can often causc us to fail. Fear of failure or rejection, for example, may prevent us from taking risks or giving our very best effort. The best way to root out fear is to redirect our thoughts—choose to think positive, powerful, and productive thoughts—and dwell on success rather than failure.

Practicing being confident is important, even acting as if we have an abundance of confidence before we actually accomplish our goal. In so doing, we create new healthy patterns and programs in our minds, which we will rely on in competitive and pressure situations.

PRACTICE: The power of words is extraordinary. Not just the ones we hear from others but the ones we speak to ourselves. How do you speak to yourself? Pick a time in the day and observe how you talk to yourself. Try this while driving to work, preparing for a meeting or a game, or otherwise getting ready to take the stage. What kind of internal dialogue do you have with yourself? Do you treat yourself as well as you treat your friends or your children?

Try talking to yourself in ways that you would talk to those who are most important to you and whom you love most in life. As you begin to work with affirmations, you will become more aware of your negative self-talk. Turn some of those negative beliefs into useful and positive affirmations. Repeat your affirmations over and over in both verbal and written form. Post them in places where you will see them.

Affirmations are simple, clear, direct, positive statements, words, or thoughts that you convey to yourself. You can say them out loud or silently. At some level, we are always talking to ourselves. The important thing is to remember to speak to ourselves as kindly as we do to others.

Montana

When it comes to performance, in sports or business, if we don't have confidence that we're going to complete a pass or make that big sale, the chances of our doing so are not good. We will have defeated ourselves before we even get into the game.

It wasn't until my second year with the 49ers, after I'd learned the moves and idiosyncrasies of my receivers, that I started throwing better in training camp and developing some real confidence in my ability to do the job. I started to believe in myself as a pro.

Bill Walsh knew what he was doing. He brought me along carefully and slowly, never throwing me into a hopelessly lost game to gain experience. Instead, he let me take over when the ball was in good field position and I had a chance to do something positive, even lead a scoring drive. Today, when I see coaches put young quarterbacks into a hopeless situation or pull them out of a game after they've made one mistake, I cringe. That is no way to help a fellow just starting out to find his confidence. Quite the opposite, it's how to break someone's confidence and ruin his spirit.

Confidence is not about having an oversize ego or displaying arrogance. I remember one young defensive back who thought he was the best pass-coverage man alive. He called himself "The Blanket." He implored the rest of us, whenever we were interviewed by the media, to be sure and mention that he was the best defensive back in football. One game, the Blanket got burned for a couple touchdowns. Afterward, he found his locker draped with a blanket that had big holes burned in it. The next game was away, and when it was time to get on the bus to go to the stadium, the Blanket refused to leave the hotel. A few days later, he was traded.

Arrogance is not confidence. If people have true inner confidence, they can't wait to get on the bus, play the game, and show what they can do. They want the ball every time. Those are the people you want on your team.

Any of us can have our confidence shaken by a series of mistakes or defeats, but no one can take it away from us. Confidence is completely ours to give to ourselves, and ours to take away when we feel low. If we've lost it, we simply have to find it again. We must fall back on the fundamentals, those things we have developed confidence in doing well. Once we get going again, we can start to take more chances, as long as we stay within our capabilities. Those fundamentals will drive us.

Whatever business I've gone into since my playing days, I've always made a point to learn the fundamentals of the new game right away, whether it's investments, real estate, or public speaking. When my two former teammates and I started our investment capital company, we knew nothing about the business. We could go out and talk to other professional athletes and line up clients to give us money to manage, but then what? We began working with the best investment advisers in the business, and we learned about the world of private equity capital. We kept it simple, learned along the way, and paid attention to fundamentals. Today we have $500 million in assets and continue to grow and offer our clients a good rate of return. Even when you follow time-tested fundamentals, there is no guarantee you won't make mistakes. It's important, however, to have confidence that you will succeed.

I'm the first to admit that I didn't have the biggest, strongest arm in the world. I knew that, so I always had to be fairly correct in my stance and balance to get the ball to go any distance. Sometimes I had to throw off balance, but it was never a far throw, I guarantee it. I had confidence in the system I was playing in, which had a lot of short- and mid-range passing routes, and I knew the fundamentals forward and backward. That gave me the confidence to do what I had to do and deliver the ball where it had to be.

I recently spoke to a college quarterback about his needing to have more confidence in himself. I noticed that he was reluctant to change plays at the line of scrimmage. If the coaches told him to call a run on second down, he would stay with it, even against an eight-man front designed to stop the run and with the defensive backs playing ten yards off the wide receivers.

"When you see something is not going to work, have the confidence to change it," I told the young quarterback. "Stand up and hit one of your receivers. You won't get yelled at by the coach for changing the play if you pick up eight yards. That's how you build your own confidence and your team's confidence in you."

At a press conference the week before last year's Super Bowl, one of the wide receivers was asked about the individual defensive backs he would be facing and how he intended to handle them. He shrugged and said he wasn't able to discuss them because he didn't know their names, nor did he care to. The reporters couldn't believe the receiver did not know his opponents.

They asked me for a comment. I don't know what they thought I would say, but my answer seemed to surprise them.

"I think that's great. You don't change what you do best to compete against someone. You can't allow someone to dictate to you how good you're going to be. Let the other guy worry about changing his game."

That is playing with true confidence in yourself.

Bill Walsh did something similar with the 49ers. He would script out the first twenty-five offensive plays before a game. This allowed us to be better prepared mentally, and it also instilled an attitude that we were going to go out and, in spite of the other team's best efforts, dictate how we would play.

Mitchell

When I was in Little League, I had a Puerto Rican coach named Phil Nigran. I was a pitcher, and whenever I'd get into a difficult situation on the mound, I'd hear Mr. Nigran in the dugout, yelling at me in his heavy accent, "Mitch, you can do it! You can do it, Mitch!" Over and over he repeated those words until they penetrated my psyche and took root at some deep level.

At the time I didn't exactly know what was happening, but as I look back, I think those often-repeated words of encouragement, *You—can—do—it,* must have helped me to build my confidence in myself.

When I got into high school, I played goalie on the soccer team. At one away game, about thirty miles from our school on a cold, rainy fall day, there was no one in the stands except for my mother sitting under her umbrella, watching and rooting for me. It was a sight I will never forget. Having her there somehow made me feel that I could conquer the world.

When I was a senior in high school, I was having a good year playing basketball. Though my dad had a big job and managed a lot of people, he always found a way to make it to my games. But then he had a heart attack and needed a surgical bypass. There was nothing routine about a bypass in those days, and we were all very scared for him. The doctor told him he must rest, stay off work— and stay away from my basketball games.

One night we were playing our archrival, and I was having a terrible game. Even though I was averaging twenty points a game that season, I couldn't shoot the ball the first half. By halftime we were behind, and I had only four points. At the beginning of the second half, I looked up in the stands and saw my father sitting way up in one corner all by himself. He had sneaked in. I knew he shouldn't be there, yet the feeling of support I got from seeing him was like a direct infusion of confidence. It took over my body. As soon as the game started again, I felt as if something special was happening. I got into a zone, launching some deep shots and hitting them. We won the game, and I finished with twenty-eight points. I went on to win all-state honors that year, and a college basketball scholarship.

Joe and I have that in common: having had very supportive parents, growing up. A healthy dose of confidence from those around us, especially in our formative years, is a gift.

At some point, though, we must find our own confidence. No one else can give it to us. It does not come from coaches, teammates, or anyone else. It comes from inside. Inner confidence is something to be learned and developed, and once we've tapped into it, we can go back and get it whenever we need it.

True confidence in oneself is specific. I can believe in myself, but that doesn't mean I have the confidence to be a professional musician or a world-champion boxer or an Olympic tennis player or anything else for which I have little or average talent or training. Belief is about being something; confidence is about doing something.

When we understand our unique gifts, evaluate our skills and our talents, and identify our strengths, we have confidence. We know the things we do well. Confidence is not magical. It is factual and a lot about repetition, focus, hard work, and desire.

I refer to inner confidence as "cellular confidence," because it can be lodged deeply in the core of peak performers. A perfect example of that is Chris Mullin, who, although retired from professional basketball for several years, is still a skilled and confident shooter. We were in my backyard playing basketball not long ago, and it got dark. I have a ball that glows in the dark, so we kept shooting around. Finally, it got so pitch-black out that we couldn't see each other, just that neon ball. Mully stepped back to three-point range and took a shot. It hit nothing but net. I rebounded the ball and passed it back. He shot again. *Swish.* We kept going like that—Mully shooting and me feeding him the ball—and he made twenty-seven consecutive three-point shots in complete darkness before he missed.

"Mully, how do you do that?" I asked. "You can't see the basket."

"You've got to be able to do your job with your eyes closed. You can't always see your goal, but you gotta know it's there, and that you can do what it takes."

That's cellular confidence.

Sometimes there's an assumption that the coach—whether in sports or in business—is the one to instill the confidence in the athlete or client. Such as, "She made me feel confident after we talked for an hour" or "He told me I did an awesome job out there today." Although that's helpful, there is a better way to build confidence. It is accomplished through the practice and execution of things we do well. At some point in our development, each of us must assume the responsibility of producing a well of inner confidence upon which to draw.

A coach or boss should expect the player or employee to find his or her own confidence, and beyond that, to instill confidence in other team members by demonstrating a particular skill to a high level of proficiency. Disgruntled athletes often complain to agents, the media, or anyone who will listen that a coach didn't show any confidence in them, so they performed badly. After years of coaching, I know that this is nothing more than an excuse.

Can anyone imagine Michael Jordan complaining that his coach didn't have confidence in him? Quite the opposite. And why do coaches show confidence in such players? Because they see that these players have the aptitude, talent, experience, and everything else it takes to get the job done. They communicate that readiness through their words and actions, all of which boost the confidence of everyone around them.

Joe once told me that most people don't remember that "The Catch" that beat the Dallas Cowboys 28–27 in the 1981 NFC championship game, and put the 49ers into their first Super Bowl, was a third-down play. It was third-and-three at the Dallas six-yard line, with fifty-eight seconds on the clock. As spectacular as that play was, if the receiver, Dwight Clark, hadn't caught the pass, Joe said he "always figured we'd score on the next down."

When a set of skills, combined with talent, meet up with a strong internal level of confidence, it's amazing what can be accomplished.

Fail Fast and Move On

EVERYONE MAKES MISTAKES, LOSES CONTESTS, AND OTHERWISE EXPERI-
ences defeat. It's part of being human. Committing errors is how
we learn to be better. Failure is an integral part of success.

Thomas Edison once told a group of reporters that he had tried
more than ten thousand materials as filaments for his new inven-
tion, the lightbulb. One reporter asked how had he been able to
remain steadfast in the face of so much failure. "Failure?" Edison
responded. "I didn't fail." What he did, he explained, was successfully eliminate ten thousand elements that did not work. In the
end, the fact that Edison failed more times, and lost more money
in unsuccessful experiments than any other inventor in modern
history, means little. He is the greatest inventor in modern history.

What one person defines as failure, another sees as an opportunity to improve. Successful people look at failure as temporary.
They don't give up; they keep trying. In contrast, people who
don't use setbacks as opportunities to learn tend to look at failure
as permanent and personal. They become stuck.

To attain our goals, we need to take setbacks in stride, retaining
a willingness and even an enthusiasm to grow beyond our comfort
zone. We must evaluate a situation in which we fall short of a goal,

identify the right and wrong of our strategy, and emerge empowered and energized for another try.

The last NFL team that went undefeated for an entire season
(1972), the Miami Dolphins, had suffered a bitter loss (24–3) to
the Dallas Cowboys in the Super Bowl the year before. That loss,
Dolphins quarterback Bob Griese believed, helped motivate and
energize the team to go 17–0 the following year, and go on to win
back-to-back Super Bowls. Learning from failure is a vital and
necessary step to achieving success.

Positive change can arise out of desperation as well as inspiration. Failure often acts as a catalyst for change and innovation,
forcing a reframing of expectations and a reevaluation of skills and
strategies.

"It may sound strange," said two-time Olympic pole vault
champion Bob Richards, "but many champions are made champions by setbacks."

On some level, each of us would like to succeed at all times in
every aspect of life, but that is unrealistic and seldom possible.

Those who never fail are those who never try. If we do anything
long enough, we will be humbled. Even when we prepare and
practice well, and have an enormous desire to succeed, we will at
times fail to reach our goal. Not every Olympian wins a medal,
and not every sports team—even those made up of the most
skilled and elite athletes in the world—wins every game.

Failure in business is particularly unwelcome. We have all heard
the old adage "Somebody's going to lose his job over this one."
Many innovative companies, however, continue to look for ways
to embrace what is called "productive failure"—failure that comes
as a result of making a well-calculated yet aggressive move to test
the market with a new product or service. Petersen Publishing, a
successful magazine company, had the walls in the lobby of its Los
Angeles headquarters filled with framed first-issue covers. The
founder, Robert Petersen, did not overthink magazine launches. If
someone had a good idea and a handful of advertisers expressed an

interest, they went for it. With each launch was the understanding that if it did not work, the title would be killed quickly, with no punishment or firings. With most companies, killing a launched product is a hard thing to do, but not at Petersen. Petersen became so good at testing new concepts that it could produce a new title at half the cost and in half the time of anyone else, and most of all, the company had learned to cut its losses quickly and early. The people at Petersen were proud of all the titles they tried. Failing fast and moving on was a core part of their culture, and they built a successful financial model around it.

The founder of IBM, Thomas Watson, Jr., knew about the culture of accepting failure as part of the cost of building an innovative company. One of his junior executives once spent $12 million on a new project that never got off the ground. When failure was apparent, he went into Watson's office with his resignation in hand. "I thought I'd save you the trouble of firing me," said the young executive. "I don't want your resignation," said Watson. "I just invested twelve million dollars in your education. Get back to work."

Many famously successful people have gone through failure and acknowledge the importance of moving past it and learning from the experience.

"I can accept failure," said Michael Jordan, one of the greatest basketball players of all time, who failed in his effort to play professional baseball. "Everyone fails at something. But I can't accept not trying."

"There are no secrets to success," said former U.S. Army general and secretary of state Colin Powell. "It is the result of preparation, hard work, and learning from failure."

Getting knocked down is no disgrace as long as we pick ourselves up. Indeed, we can succeed from our failures.

PRACTICE #1: Write down the biggest setback or lowest point you have experienced in your career, sports, school, or life in general. With each setback, one learns a lesson. What are the lessons you have learned from yours? What mistakes were made? Why did they happen? How could they have been prevented? How can you do better next time? What changes did you make?

PRACTICE #2: Choose a sport or hobby to focus on that will stretch your concept of failure. Try something you don't have to do well in. Whatever you choose, give yourself permission to fail miserably. It might be going bowling for the first time in years, and laughing at all the gutter balls. Contemplate the failure. Notice how you respond physically and emotionally to your perceived "failure."

In this one targeted and specific area, you have generated a field of permission and acceptance. Failure should be out in the open. When failure is restricted to an unimportant area of your life, you may be surprised by how fun and relaxing it can be to fail—and find yourself going back for more. That is the essence of failing fast and moving on.

Montana

Football is a great place to learn how to fail.

Not long ago, I was at a sports memorabilia convention, and one of those guys who has memorized every imaginable statistic came up to me. "Say, Joe, do you realize that the first pass you threw in a professional game was intercepted? And the last pass you threw in a game was intercepted, too."

After thinking about it, I realized the guy was right.

My first start in the NFL was against Seattle, and I threw an interception that was returned for a touchdown. Then it got worse. I threw another interception, and the defender ran over me on his way into the end zone. We lost 48–0. As for that last interception, it was a slant pattern, and the receiver stopped running. The ball was intercepted in the end zone. If I had known that would be my last pass, I would have been a lot more upset. Regardless, my sixteen-year pro football career was sandwiched between two spectacular failures.

As if screwing up on the field before sixty thousand screaming fans and millions of viewers on TV wasn't enough, come Monday, we filed into the film room and watched our mistakes all over again—repeatedly and in slow motion. Our errors were pointed out to us by the coaches in excruciating detail, often accompanied by howls from our teammates, who knew their turn could be just a few plays away. I used to dread going into the room, but I learned to handle criticism and not to be thin-skinned.

We didn't go into the film room to see what we did right. Even in games we won, there were plenty of mistakes to review. We needed to learn what we did wrong, so as not to repeat the same miscues week in and week out. You can't learn how to get better if you don't understand what you did wrong.

Bill Walsh understood that everyone makes mistakes. Today too many coaches pull young players out of the game when they make mistakes. In football, the game happens so fast, we're all bound to fumble or make a mistake in the course of a game. Coach Walsh didn't mind if you messed up or had a bad game once in a while, but he didn't want the same mistakes being made consistently, week to week. If that happened, he'd call a player into his office. Sometimes they would go over film. "Look, here's what has been happening," Coach Walsh would say. "We've got to find a way to change it."

Come game time, though, you had to leave behind your past mistakes. If I was thinking about a mistake I made on the previous play when we broke the huddle, I couldn't concentrate on what I had to do next.

As a junior at Notre Dame, I went in for our starting quarterback when we were down 24–14. I was scared and had every right to be. I hadn't thrown a pass in a game in two years. Not wanting my teammates to know how nervous I was, I thought the best way to calm down was to call for a simple, short pass to our tight end on my first play. When I let go of the ball, it flew—well, more like flapped—through the air like a wounded duck. It went end over end, and it was underthrown on top of it. It should have been intercepted. Now I had an even bigger hole to crawl out of. I'm sure at that point not many guys in the huddle expected anything good to happen the rest of the game with me at the helm, but we started moving downfield. As we did, I grew more relaxed and confident and began hitting my receivers. We won the game, and in a real sense, I launched my Notre Dame career that day.

In subsequent games, I would discover that there was nothing worse than starting a game with an interception. What was I to do for the rest of the game? Not throw the ball? If I didn't, I would be zero for one, which was terrible. Of course I had to get over the interception, get past my mistake, and take another shot. Football is like life—you have to keep doing it in order to move ahead. Even when you miss a few passes in a row, you have to keep trying. Your teammates might be thinking something is really wrong today, and at the same time you can be having your own doubts.

But a quarterback, like any leader, must project a positive attitude and self-confidence in the huddle. Otherwise all is lost.

On that last drive against Dallas that culminated in "The Catch," I had missed another receiver, Freddie Solomon, who was open on the previous play and would have scored the go-ahead touchdown. Right there, with only fifty-eight seconds left, I could have lost us the game. The word that passed through my mind was "choke." I knew if the drive stalled after moving the ball over eighty yards downfield, and we failed to score and lost the game, we would be just another bunch of choke artists. Dallas called time-out to discuss their defensive options, and I walked over to the 49ers sideline.

Coach Walsh was talking into his headset to our coaches in the press box. When he finished, he looked at me. He warned me to be cautious. It was only third down, and if we missed on the next play, we would still have one more chance. Then he told me he wanted another pass play.

By then I had eliminated the missed pass from my thoughts. Had I dwelled on it, I may well have lost confidence in my ability to get the job done. The previous pass easily could have been picked off. Was I going to throw tentatively to avoid that possibility? Absolutely not.

I knew Coach Walsh was right. We had two chances to score. I went into the huddle, called the play, and dropped back. All my practice and training kicked in. I concentrated on finding an open receiver and throwing a catchable ball, or, if no one was open, throwing the ball out of bounds.

And there, down the field, I saw my old buddy Dwight Clark. Dwight had been afraid he wasn't going to make the team in training camp, and I'd thrown him about a thousand passes after hours to improve his catching skills. I could see him streaking across the back of the end zone, looking my way. I didn't make the best throw, but we would not be called chokers, and I would not be blamed for losing the game. Not that day, anyway.

And yes, the next day at practice, I did have to watch the film of my missing an open Freddie Solomon—in slow motion, forward and backward.

It's hard to do anything if you're worried about your next mistake. When you think about bad things that have happened or could happen, your mind is not where it should be: on this play, right here, right now. We win some bad games and lose some good games, and we have to find a way to put all of them, good or bad, behind us.

Of course, after too many failures, you sometimes need to see the handwriting on the wall and move right into something else. After retirement, I took up competitive horse jumping, a brand-new sport for me but one that Jennifer was active in. As my riding began to improve, the heights of the jumps increased, as did the difficulty of the courses. I pushed myself to get better and compete against top riders. One day, sitting in the stands after a couple of difficult rounds, I overheard two women talking.

"Did you see Joe Montana out there today?"

"Yes. I can't believe he fell off again."

I laughed, but I knew it was time to move on. I gave up jumping and took up western cutting horses, now a favorite pastime. I'm falling a lot less these days, and I've even won some competitions. I'm glad I put failure in one thing behind me so I could move on to something more enjoyable and less painful.

Mitchell

Most of the time, we do not try to fail or play to lose, even in casual contests with friends. But inevitably, we will meet defeat; we'll taste it, know it, and absorb it. Since we all fail, we might as well learn how to fail well. Successful people not only fail regularly, they are masters at handling it.

Failure is failure only when we let it negatively impact on our future performance, or allow it to keep us from attempting new activities. A winning person does neither, only learning from it.

If we play not to lose, we will lose more often than if we play to win. This is not as easy as it sounds. Many times we still have the memory of defeat and, even worse, the memory of physical or emotional pain. To possess the winning spirit, we must train ourselves to keep an eye on the goal, to stay positive, enthusiastic, and confident, while always being aware of the pitfalls and challenges we face.

In my coaching of executives and corporate teams, I have found that many businesses don't do well with failure. Employees are afraid of losing a job, a budget, and even enduring the public humiliation that can accompany business failure. While repeated failure is never acceptable, much of my coaching practice is designed to help individuals face head-on those fears of failure—to get past them so they can exert new energy to succeed.

One technology company I coached had a no-failure culture, if not policy. One missed major obstacle, one major operational hiccup, and pack your bags. Executives had learned to keep their objectives small and their bases covered. The cost came in the form of reduced innovation and less passion in the ranks. I began coaching individuals to learn to identify those projects they believed in and were so passionate about that they would be willing to lose their job over them. These projects became their lines in the sand. Scared players changed into power players, individuals totally committed to their work. Soon individuals were being driven to the jobs and responsibilities that best matched their skills and passion, and innovation once again flourished throughout the company. We also used the "fail fast" model to break down unwieldy, complex challenges into manageable projects, reducing the risk of a big failure while creating opportunities for small setbacks and learning along the way.

In training for success, we shouldn't hide from failure. Just like football players in the film room, we study failure. We want to see how it happens and which strategies will work to keep us from making the same mistake again. The speed with which we shift from that place of underachieving or failure to a place of confidence and achievement is crucial to achieving our own level of greatness.

In sports, all champions and championship teams lose from time to time. The lesson is that losing is not a permanent defeat but something from which they can profit. Athletes are taught, more than most people, how to learn from their mistakes, knowing they will soon be back competing in the same activity where they may have lost the day before.

In business as well, we should avoid beating ourselves up over mistakes from the past. The benefits of forgiving ourselves, letting go of blame, and not being so hard on ourselves far surpass the negative effects of personal condemnation. We almost always get a second chance to accomplish what defeated us, but with an understanding of what went wrong previously.

In coaching talented, competitive executives, I sometimes find individuals who are facing major failure for the first time in their forties and fifties. In some cases, I find that the confidence of prior success has encouraged them to stray too far from their sweet spot of core skills, capabilities, expertise, or even areas of passion. Sometimes it's caused by the intoxicant of more power, or, in the case of the Internet boom, the opportunity to create tremendous wealth. Frequently, despite massive effort, extensive experience, and personal sacrifice, short-term failure is inevitable in business.

In these cases, I coach recovery—always back to the basics, practicing the skills, demonstrating foundational strengths, and rebuilding confidence. The idea is to quickly diagnose the root cause of the situation and reach out to mentors and others who have the individual's best interests at heart. These failures, however painful, can be the seeds of discovery and rediscovery. They force introspection and redirect focus to areas of passionate interest. "Back to the core" is the key to overcoming failure.

Sugar Ray Leonard, the former world boxing champion, shared with me his experiences of failure when we met during family vacations in Hawaii. Talking about all aspects of performance, he said the advantage of losing is that it builds a "mental toughness for the next fight in the ring and in life." He was always conscious, he told me, of building up his "inner reservoir" so he could call on it when he needed it. Part of his reservoir came from learning how to overcome earlier losses in the ring.

Failing or losing is not the way we plan things. How we handle the unexpected—dealing with something less than perfect—reveals more about our fortitude than about our success. How do we train ourselves to become more capable when things don't go our way? When we're not having a good day? We do so by being bigger than our performance. We don't fit our lives into our performances; we fit our performances into our lives. If we're totally dependent upon our performances for our self-esteem and validation, then we will be consumed by failure. That's why it's vital to think bigger, to find valuable pieces of ourselves and our lives that transcend performance on the playing field or at work. Whenever I coach this point, I tell my clients, "We're now entering into the realm of the spirit and the soul."

We have to be tough enough on ourselves to analyze our performance honestly. Yet we also have to love and be kind to ourselves—such as giving ourselves permission to miss a goal from time to time. Sometimes we have to go through a negative stretch of time, perhaps voicing a few choice words or an outburst of emotional frustration. Do it if you need to, but remember that it's important to return with a more supportive and gentle approach, reaffirming that we still believe in what we're doing, and that we'll be okay after we've made some adjustments.

In its purest form, failure is essential for achieving excellence.

PART TWO

Heart of a Team

Heart of a Team

WE BELIEVE THE WORD "TEAM" IS OVERUSED IN CORPORATE AMERICA. Just because a group of people work together does not make them a team, even if they are employed by the same firm or wear the same uniform.

A team is more than a group of people working together. To be a real team, there must be a team spirit, with each person genuinely caring about his or her teammates' success. There must be a willingness to help bring out the best in others to achieve the same goal.

Sometimes in discussions about corporate team building, people will make analogies of business to family and military experience. Neither works well. Family life need not be goal-oriented at all—other than supporting each other and enjoying each other's company—and combat metaphors comparing an office to a foxhole or a deal to a battle seem shallow and disrespectful.

A winning team is not dependent on the external environment—the office, facility, or arena. A winning team is dependent on the people who work in that environment. Success is not about a team's technical resources; it's about the human resources. In business, many companies have the same computers, communication devices, copy machines, desks, and even the same products and competitors. In professional sports, every team comprises excellent athletes who have the same equipment and training available to them. So why do some teams fail while others succeed?

What distinguishes one team from another is the feeling of a special connection that each member has with the others: trust, commitment, inspiration, consideration, attitude, communication, leadership. Teams that win have chemistry and synergy, with members focusing on doing their own job well and assisting others whenever they can.

The five principles in this section define the essence of excellent teamwork, providing examples of how to apply our individual skills to a larger circle of influence. Whether we choose a team or it chooses us, how do we personally perform and contribute to improve that team? How do we surrender our personal agenda for the larger goal? How do we bring out the best in others?

A successful team is constantly fighting and winning the battle over selfishness, a difficult and noble feat to achieve. Let's face it: We all have our personal agendas. To surrender our individual ego to the good of a team takes work, sacrifice, trust, and courage.

As Tommy Lasorda, former manager of the Los Angeles Dodgers, once said, "My responsibility is to get twenty-four guys playing for the name on the front of their shirts and not the one on the back."

Cultivate the Right Attitude

A POSITIVE, CONFIDENT, AND CARING ATTITUDE LIES AT THE HEART OF the winning spirit. A healthy attitude can be contagious, but none of us should wait around to catch it from someone else. It should be a priority for everyone to have a positive attitude throughout the day, at work and at home. Often we will receive from others the very attitude—good or bad—that we project. When we see good in others and praise them for it, they will do the same.

Our attitude toward one another can either enhance or destroy the momentum of an individual or a group. We have all had an exciting goal or idea we were working on and shared it with someone who in turn reacted negatively, pointing out all the things wrong about it and how hard it would be for us to accomplish. Your enthusiasm is shattered, which can be paralyzing. And in turn, your own attitude about work sours.

Most of us spend more waking hours at work than at home, and yet public opinion surveys reveal that the majority of us do not like our jobs. What we dislike has a lot to do with *attitude*—emanating from management, coworkers, customers, and even ourselves.

One experienced executive coach makes a point of having clients who are unhappy, irritable, and pessimistic begin each day with a verbal affirmation. Upon awakening and before rising from bed, they are to repeat to themselves, "Today is a great day!" Then, during their morning shower: "I am wide-awake and ready to be my best." Some are cynical in the beginning and think the exercise is foolish, but nearly all who practice improving their state of mind actually do so. Their attitude shifts to feeling more relaxed, positive, and optimistic.

Becoming aware of our own attitude is critical, because once we recognize how powerful our mental state is and how it influences everything we do, we can change it. We understand that if our attitude is not contributing to our company, team, family, or personal success or happiness, then something needs to change. That something is ourselves.

If personal change is required, we may need to renew our enthusiasm for life by focusing on all that is good and possible. We may need to develop the attitude that what we do matters and makes a difference in the lives of others.

A single person with a powerful attitude can impact team chemistry in an incredible way. One person with courage, determination, confidence, and skill can often bring out those same traits in team members who perhaps had those qualities all along.

It is sometimes difficult to be the most optimistic person on a team. It can feel embarrassing and lonely to be a positive light in a sea of cynics. No one says that being a positive force on a team is an easy job, but someone needs to step up and be that person. Why not you?

When several team members choose to take on the responsibility and commitment to develop a positive attitude, great things happen. Hurtful gossip may be eliminated in the workplace or new lines of communication opened between fellow workers. One player can ignite the team with spirit and enthusiasm, bringing out the best in the other players.

Since our attitude plays a huge part in the success of our business, sports, and personal life, it is only common sense that we work hard to develop a great attitude. We give ourselves permission to ask for and expect the best from ourselves and from life, knowing with quiet confidence that we have what it takes to make our dreams come true. We train ourselves to look for the good in situations and in other people, believing that positive energy can be found everywhere, in everyone. When you create a world-class attitude, everyone will want to be your teammate.

PRACTICE: Stress in all of its many forms, good or bad, can jostle us into looking at something with a different and expanded perspective, or it can take us down into a pit of despair. It's important to monitor our stress levels in all areas of life, and find ways to blow off steam when needed, such as engaging ourselves in activities that are energizing, easy to accomplish, and scheduled regularly.

To trigger an attitude change, call a temporary time-out. Move your physical body to another location, or engage your mind with a different focus, such as reading a book, listening to uplifting music, or exercising.

Another strategy to facilitate a change in attitude is to put yourself in a different environment to call forth another aspect of yourself. For instance, go watch children playing on a playground, or attend a concert with accomplished musicians, or hang out with someone who is naturally energized and passionate about life, or find a way to give back and volunteer at a charity. Whatever you do, introduce an interruption in your habitual way of doing things and thinking about life.

Montana

"The heart of a team" became our saying one year on the 49ers. It was suggested by Ronnie Lott, one of the hardest-hitting defensive backs ever to play the game. Ronnie, who became the leader of our defense during our big years, kept saying we needed to embrace the attitude that we all had "only one heartbeat." Some fifty guys were going after the same goal—to win the Super Bowl—which we could achieve only together, as a team.

The mantra caught on in the locker room and on the field. Ronnie talked about it the whole year: "We all have one heartbeat," he kept saying. "It's not offense. It's not defense. It's not special teams. It's not a coach or a bunch of coaches. It's all of us *together.*"

Everyone got it. Our collective attitude—that we were all in this thing together—inspired us. We knew there would be ups and downs during the season, but as long as we stayed on the same path and kept the common goal and helped one another succeed whenever and however we could, we would win our share of games. That year—with one heartbeat—we won the Super Bowl. The first frame of our highlight film for the year reads: ONE HEART-BEAT.

It is amazing to see one guy like Ronnie Lott pass along his attitude and enthusiasm to an entire football team. I saw Jerry Rice do it, too, when he ran those passes he caught in practice all the way into the end zone. The veteran receivers ribbed him for such rookie behavior, but a funny thing happened. It became contagious. I'd throw the ball to John Taylor, and there he was, running for a touchdown in practice. Roger Craig would catch one, and all three of them would run to the end zone. It started out just for fun, but then something changed. The other guys saw how hard Jerry was willing to work, and everyone else wanted to work that hard, too, and show how they were willing to sacrifice for the team. Pretty soon the defensive backs started running all the way with the receivers to the end zone, trying to stop them. The entire team caught a dose of Jerry's work ethic.

I have often been asked what really goes on in a huddle during a big game. That's one place they haven't yet put cameras or microphones, and it's probably a good thing. The huddle is the place where the attitude of the quarterback is most important, as other players key off it. I always tried to be as positive as I could be, regardless of the circumstances, in addition to prepared and focused. Loose and upbeat helped, too.

In the 1989 Super Bowl, our offense was having a tough day. The Bengals were all over us, even reading our audibles. It seemed as though they knew what we were going to do before we did. I began to wonder if it was hopeless. I had a feeling my teammates might be wondering the same thing. We were behind 16–13 with 3:10 left in the game and possession of the ball on our own eight-yard line.

We went into our huddle. Some of the guys seemed tense, especially Harris Barton, a talented offensive tackle who had a tendency to be uptight. Looking up from where I was kneeling, I saw between two of my linemen the actor John Candy standing on the sideline eating popcorn. "Look, isn't that John Candy?" I said. Harris looked over. So did some of the other guys. Then they turned back and looked at me like I was crazy. We all laughed. The tension had been broken. I called the next two plays, and we began an eleven-play, ninety-three-yard drive to score the winning touchdown with thirty-four seconds left in the game.

Whether it comes from inspiration—like Lott's "one heartbeat"—or intensity and drive—like Rice's work ethic—or just a needed laugh at a key time in a huddle, attitude is contagious among teammates. Often you just need one person or one positive act to get the momentum going your way.

Mitchell

Entering a deli in my hometown one day, I passed two people on their way out. One said to the other, "I really want to have Mary on my team for this project." The other said, "You betcha. I always want Mary on my team." I wondered what Mary must be like, and what special attitude she possessed to be considered such a prized team member.

Bringing a positive attitude to our team means we are committed and enthusiastic. We bring energy to everything we do. We are open to listening well to others and willing to consider new ideas. We make no excuses for what happened yesterday; instead, we give our full effort to the present.

I love to coach people who are driven to improve their attitude. They know that a positive attitude is essential to success and happiness, and they understand that they ultimately get back what they give to others.

I ask my clients questions such as: "What kind of attitude do you want to project to the world?" "Do you want to be known for your courage and enthusiasm?" "Do you want to be seen as a sincere, honest, committed leader?" "Do you want to be known as a practical, no-nonsense, tough-minded manager? Or would you rather be known for your creativity and compassion?"

Nobody possesses all the qualities of a positive attitude. None of us is perfect. We all have areas to work on. But we do have the choice of how much or little we want to influence others in our sphere—a smile, a compliment to someone who needs it, an expression of optimism. All of these thoughts and actions go out into the world and come back to us in kind, many times over.

There are three attitudes that are difficult to coach and deal with in a teammate: greed, self-centeredness, and arrogance. They show up in a variety of ways, all of them damaging to the team, as well as to other individuals. Like a positive attitude, they, too, can spread and infect a team.

In sports, it's easy to recognize a player consumed with his or her statistics, such as points scored and minutes played. Whether the team wins or loses, these players' individual numbers are always more important. They don't celebrate the individual successes of others or even the team's success.

Arrogance is another difficult attitude to crack in coaching. When a person feels a level of superiority or displays an "I am more important than you" attitude, it is difficult to get him or her to see that we are all important in our own way.

To be a great leader—whether a point guard on a championship basketball team or a top executive leading a dynamic company—it is necessary to possess an attitude and spirit of understanding and project humility and compassion for individuals from all levels of education, talent, and income.

When I think about attitude sweeping through a team, a company or even an industry, I tend to recall my work coaching technology executives during the dot-com boom in Silicon Valley. I worked mostly with bright young men who were, at least on paper, worth millions of dollars. As I worked one-on-one with them, their ethics and attitudes fascinated me.

Granted, there were a few exceptions, but what I saw was predominantly a dangerous mix of two attitudes: fear and arrogance. They were fearful about how not to lose their money, how to hang on until they could exercise their options and get out with their wealth intact. Holding on to their money seemed way more important than figuring out how to manage their employees, who depended on their leadership and vision.

I heard these executives make statements such as "We have reinvented business," "This is the new economy," and "Check your prior experience at the door." As they said that, they looked at the calendar worriedly, counting the days until they could cash in their options. This mix of arrogance and fear was a toxic cocktail of attitudes. It even affected me. Driving home from these sessions, I actually felt as if I had been poisoned or brainwashed. I wondered, Is this the new model of financial success?

Most of these young dot-com entrepreneurs were highly educated, talented, and creative. They were basically good guys. Yet this contagious attitude of fear and newfound arrogance had somehow corroded their mind-set. When the stock market imploded, where were the fundamentals that held the teams and companies together?

Recently, as I was coaching members of a large real estate company, I asked one branch manager why he had chosen to work for this particular company. He told me about an experienced agent who had come in looking for a job. The manager wasn't sure there was a place for her, so he called the general manager to see what he thought. Rather than ask how much revenue this agent could bring to the company, the general manager first wanted to know, "What kind of person is she?"

"That's why I work here," the branch manager explained. "When you find a work environment where the attitude is—from the top down—that people come first, there's nowhere else I want to go."

Lead by Example

THE SINGLE MOST POTENT TOOL FOR INSPIRING OTHERS TO STRIVE FOR excellence is leading by example: teaching by our actions, following our own advice, and doing whatever we would ask of others.

Exceptional leadership requires integrity and respect. Effective leaders speak the truth. They understand that if their actions come in direct conflict with their words, the impact of their message will be lessened. Walking the talk is essential.

An outstanding leader helps others embrace their unique position on the team, and the specific responsibilities that come with that position. On a successful team, everyone's contribution is needed, valued, and integrated into the team's goals. Leadership demands trust, honesty, communication, and service. A leader projecting these traits influences the team in the most powerful way possible: by example. Leading by example is inspired leadership. Such leadership is more influential than motivating through fear, intimidation, or coercion, which can be dispiriting to everyone.

Furthermore, great leaders are willing to receive feedback from many sources, either up or down the organizational ladder. They are open to feedback, and they realize that no one can know everything, no matter how far up the ladder they have moved. The notion of giving, receiving, and asking for feedback in an open, honest, and sincere manner is one of the most powerful things a leader can do to impact high performance and create change and growth in people.

One large company's major division was struggling under the leadership of a veteran executive. There was increasing discord between him and those on his team, many of whom had stopped respecting him. The CEO, concerned about the situation, listened to the perspective of the executive, then made a few suggestions for immediate improvements to team morale, including asking for and listening to feedback. The CEO wanted to help this otherwise talented executive be successful, and he certainly didn't want to see anyone on his team fail. But the executive wanted no part of anyone else's ideas—not from those on his team, not even from his boss. The CEO looked the executive in the eye and said, "Tell me, how old were you when you realized that you knew everything?" There was, of course, no good answer to the question. The executive's limitations had much more to do with his leadership shortcomings than his business acumen, and he eventually had to be let go.

Every leader needs to develop the willingness to solicit and accept challenging feedback. Smart and effective leaders know how to pose revealing questions, then listen well to the responses. They know that ultimately, they are not in control of anyone. They can lead the way through example, but in truth they depend upon those they are leading to get the job done. Phil Jackson, the legendary NBA coach with nine championship rings, never scored one point as a coach. His players did the actual work. Yet because of his coaching methods and his ability to manage some of the best basketball talent of all time, *Sports Illustrated* named him the best NBA coach of the past fifty years.

Although natural leaders tend to stand out early, other individuals learn how to lead over time. Vincent Lombardi once said,

"Leaders are not born. Leaders are made, and they are made by effort and hard work." An effective leader willingly takes on responsibility and possesses a high degree of mental toughness. Any leader will at some point hear criticism, endure mistakes, and bear losses.

John Polumbo, the president and CEO of AT&T Consumer, who has led several multinational companies over the past two decades, recently explained what he had learned about how to be an effective leader. "It comes down to sharing big and sharing a lot," he said. "And always be sure to give away the credit and take the blame."

PRACTICE: Identify one person (or more) in your life who best demonstrates leading by example. Make a list of qualities this person possesses. Circle the qualities you also notice in yourself, and which you put into practice on a consistent basis. Highlight the qualities that you do not possess or practice frequently. Choose from the highlighted list one quality that you will focus on and practice in the next thirty days. Don't tell anyone you are doing this self-improvement exercise. The goal is to work on developing this quality so much that at least one person in your life comments to you on your success. Write in your performance journal what you have chosen to improve, as well as those qualities that you believe you regularly and successfully put into action.

Montana

It's no secret why Jerry Rice and Ronnie Lott became the leaders they did on the 49ers. Both of them led from way out in front, and by their own example, expecting nothing more of their teammates than what they themselves were willing to put on the line each and every time they suited up.

I will never forget the crushing sound of Ronnie slamming full speed into runners and blockers, and separating ball carriers from footballs. It made for some awesome sound effects. No opponent who met Lott shoulder-to-shoulder on a football field ever forgot the meeting. Once asked to describe his style of delivering a defensive blow or tackle, Ronnie said, "It comes from your toes and from your soul. It comes from all that you are."

Ronnie was always the first one to lay it on the line, and he never backed down from anything. One season, he partially tore off his left pinkie finger at the second knuckle when it got caught in someone's shoulder pads during a game. The doctors recommended surgery to sew on the fingertip and said Ronnie would miss six weeks. He asked how long he would be out if they amputated the fingertip. No time at all, he was told. "Cut it off," he said. They did, and he played. How could you *not* want this man on your team?

No one can be a leader by words alone, not in the NFL, the NBA, or any other profession I can think of. It's hard to believe in someone who sits back and directs from afar. A real leader works as hard and as well as he wants others to work. He sacrifices as much as any other member of the team.

In any sport, it's not enough to be driven to succeed personally. You need to bring everyone else on your team along with you. I've seen this sign in football locker rooms: GOOD PLAYERS INSPIRE THEMSELVES, GREAT PLAYERS INSPIRE OTHERS. The great leaders in sports all have one thing in common: When they were in the game, they made their teammates better players.

If people think they're better than the team, or above everyone else, they aren't going to earn their teammates' respect. No one individual should take credit for what is happening. Sharing the credit is important if a team is going to work together and win.

It's also important to understand that as a leader, you cannot be the best friend of everyone on the team, because a leader must deliver unpleasant messages at times. It's respect a leader needs most, not popularity.

Mitchell

Like the true team player he is, Joe generously gives credit to Ronnie Lott and Jerry Rice for being leaders on the team of the 1980s. But there was another guy on that team who did the very same thing. He wore number 16.

When Lott was inducted into the Pro Football Hall of Fame in Canton, Ohio, he gave his own share of credit. In his induction speech, he called Joe Montana "a giant of a man," explaining that he "set an example for me and our team." Speaking directly to Joe, who was in the audience, Lott added, "Joe, you gave me the courage to face adversity, the courage to face pain. You taught me never to give up."

Joe embodies the winning spirit not through all the Super Bowl rings he owns, but in the way he led by example. He has spent most of his life leading by example. He, too, laid it on the line every time and never backed down. Joe was not only able to do his own job; he was also able to lead and inspire others to do their jobs.

Not every team member has to be what I call the "guardian of the team." Not everyone has the ability to mobilize others, inspiring them to contribute to victory. Having a few—or even just one—per team is all that's necessary to win. All the great quarterbacks, point guards, and CEOs have had the stuff to be the guardian of the team. Their reach extends beyond their arms. They are able to embrace the entire team and infuse individuals with confidence and verve.

Whenever I think of someone who led by example, my thoughts go to a young man I coached on my junior college basketball team, Kevin Koch. His teammates elected him captain of the team. During that session, I asked everyone to write down on a slip of paper their personal and team goals for the season, and then I read them all back. Kevin's slip had only one goal, and it fit into both categories: "I want to help everyone reach their goals." I knew then that the players had chosen the right man to lead them. Ironically—or perhaps not—Kevin achieved the most individual success on the team that year. He went on to win a full scholarship to play basketball at a four-year college.

Leaders less concerned with taking the credit for success are often the most successful. These leaders give away credit and praise, graciously accepting criticism even when it may not be theirs. Good managers care about both the results and the people responsible for the results.

Good leaders also possess a spirit of abundance. They always see opportunities and unlocked possibilities. Those who operate out of a feeling of scarcity never demonstrate great leadership. For them, there is never enough talent, money, or opportunity to fulfill everyone's needs. Small victories are hoarded as if there will never be enough to go around.

Abundance is not blind optimism. Abundant leaders can be shrewd and make tough decisions. But those who think abundantly emit a confidence that they and their team can rise to future challenges. They inspire others around them to be equally giving with their time, skills, and talents.

Once, when I was coaching basketball, we were in the midst of an undefeated conference season. I invited my graduate school provost to come to the game to observe my coaching style. When I saw him after the game, I anticipated his complimentary words—we had won the game—but instead, he asked me a question: "Thomas, do you care more about the game or the people playing the game?" It stopped me in my tracks.

Perhaps he had seen in me an imbalance, focusing too much on the externals—the score, our record, the standings—and putting less focus and care on the players themselves. The provost had always cautioned against using players or employees as chess pieces; rather, he advocated coaching or leading from a position where you always had their best interests at heart. I evaluated my priorities and realized I needed to spend more time developing them as young men and not just as basketball players.

Every leader should occasionally ask himself or herself these sorts of questions: "Why are you in a position of leadership?" "Have you chosen to be in a leadership role because you have a genuine urge to help develop other people?" "Do you enjoy building teams and working closely with others to attain their goals?"

I like to ask business leaders to articulate what it takes to be a powerful lead-by-example leader. A common thread that emerges is being familiar with the individual talents and gifts that make up the team. Leaders who spend the time to understand what motivates and inspires each team member will be seen as people who care.

Once, during my coaching days, I discovered that three of my players had wonderful singing voices. Two of them sang in the high school choir, and the third one had a wonderful voice without formal training. I asked them to sing the national anthem before our home games. They were dressed in their basketball uniforms, and with the stands filled, they sang their hearts out. It touched the fans as well as their fellow players. Those two minutes before each game gave us more unity, spirit, and brotherhood than anything else we did that year. Ultimately, they translated into our playing better basketball.

Remember the "I" in "Team"

STRONG TEAMS ARE COMPOSED OF STRONG INDIVIDUALS.

Excellent team performance is usually preceded by intense personal preparation, which is the responsibility of each individual member.

The "I" here is not about emphasizing a "me first" attitude. Rather, it is about each team member accepting personal accountability. Individual responsibility has long been the cornerstone of human achievement, indeed, of civilization itself. That does not change when we join a team. Each member is responsible for delivering his or her own special gifts to the team each and every day, whether in sports or business.

As team members, we must understand and embrace not only the role our physical actions and skills play in contributing to a team's success, but also our words and attitude. Courageous conversations are sometimes required—speaking the truth to our teammates and, in turn, listening when they speak the truth to us. Avoiding an issue that needs to be discussed can create strife among team members. Good teams communicate well; great teams communicate even better.

Individuals should keep sight of why they joined the team, what keeps them on the team, and what unique skills they offer the team. Conducting regular self-evaluations helps with individual performance as well as team success. Ask yourself what contribution you have made today or this week, and how you could contribute more tomorrow or next week.

In the mid-1980s, after one of the last games of the season, a sports reporter asked basketball great Larry Bird about his summer plans. Bird explained that he would be spending the summer working on his left hand, which he felt needed improvement. That season Bird would win the league MVP award, but he still wanted to improve. The following year he won MVP again. In a real sense, Bird had conducted his own personal scouting report, gaining a realistic understanding of his strengths and weaknesses.

We should all conduct our own regular scouting report. Athletes, particularly at the professional level, understand that there is a constant review and critique from the media, management, and coaches, as well as their teammates. The same is true for almost all of the performing arts. A self-scouting report helps us understand thoroughly where we possess great confidence, moderate confidence, and where we need improvement.

The ego does not always let us make honest and detached observations about our performance skills. It's amazing how many high-level athletes and executives struggle to admit weakness. We may know deep down, but it takes courage to look in the mirror and say, "This is who I am, my weaknesses as well as my strengths."

Once we are clear on where we need improvement, we have given ourselves immediate homework. If we are really serious and have that burn for greatness, we will know—as Larry Bird did— what skills we need to work on today in order to get better for tomorrow.

PRACTICE: Write down one team you are currently on—sports, family, or work. Make a list of those functions for which the team relies on you to be at your best. What are the qualities, skills, creativity, and attitudes that only you can bring? If in doubt, ask a trusted friend or family member, "What do you count on me for?" Be aware of and embrace your individual contributions to each team.

Montana

I've heard people say, "There's no 'I' in 'team.' " To be successful, they argue, it must be a team effort. There is, however, an "I" smack in the middle of "win." And to win as a team, you need individuals.

On the 49ers, our success was directly attributed to the way we prepared as individuals first, then as an organization. Each one of us needed to be responsible for ourselves. Even in football, the most team-oriented sport, it often comes down to individual effort. It is how each of us prepares that makes our team better. That's a key to team success.

This doesn't mean that any one of us is bigger than the team. All teams are made up of individuals, and ultimately, it is up to each individual to "bring it." I am responsible every day to bring my energy, my commitment, and my willingness to improve. Everyone on a team should be prepared to ask the same question: "If not I, then who?"

Only by doing it for ourselves can we be the best possible teammate. The winning spirit doesn't have time for team members who feel victimized or sorry for themselves. Our own success is a choice we make, and we have to create our own opportunity and fortune. We cannot wait for it to find us.

Another question every team member should be asking is: "What can I be doing to make myself better?" To put it another way: "What do I lack in skills that would make me better?" How do we know where we need improvement if we don't take a hard look at ourselves? We also have to know our strengths. If we don't, how can we play to our strengths? In return for working hard to make ourselves better, we are also making our team better.

I was asked at a recent seminar before a business group if I had done anything to prepare my replacement, Steve Young, to take over as starting quarterback. I said no.

"Why not?" the questioner asked.

"Because getting him ready was not my job. It was Steve's job, and the coaches'. And anyway, why should I prepare someone to take my job? It was my job to play so well that I kept Steve off the field."

Admittedly, deep down inside, I always played for myself—wanting to realize my potential and be as good as I believed I could be. And of course, I always had that desire to complete every pass and win every game. In addition to playing for my family, I played for my teammates—the guys I saw making sacrifices in practice and on the field. I played hard, I played hurt, and I played in pain because I wanted to give everything I had for the team.

In football, especially, you have to rely on your teammates. It's the ultimate team sport. A football player can reach his full potential only with the support of his teammates. In basketball, one great player can be drafted and turn a franchise from a doormat to a play-off team overnight. That doesn't often happen in football, where one man missing an assignment or running the wrong pattern can be the difference between the success and failure of a play—maybe the game.

At times I feel I get too much individual credit for things I did in my career, like engineering the scoring drive that beat the Bengals in the 1982 Super Bowl. No one talks much about the protection I received from my linemen or the patterns the receivers ran or the plays that Bill Walsh called. I did what was expected of me, but so did my teammates.

Only when individuals are ready to play can the team win.

Mitchell

Shortly after I graduated from college, my father and brother were building a home on the Jersey Shore. They asked me if I wanted a summer job helping them. They told me it would be a chance to learn some of the basics of carpentry and get paid. I said sure.

One day my brother, a master carpenter, cut a bunch of sixteen-inch studs to put between the beams before the walls and floors went in. Fire blocks, he called them; they would help maintain the integrity of the structure in the event of a fire. You had to nail each of the short ones in between two longer studs. He told me to get them all in place by lunchtime.

There were quite a few of them, enough for the entire third floor.

When lunch rolled around, I was running a little behind, so I took all the blocks and jammed them in without nailing them, knowing it would look okay and I'd get to finish when I returned from lunch.

Before I returned from lunch, my brother went up on the third floor to look at the roof rafters. He stepped on one of the loose blocks that he assumed I had nailed in place. He slipped and nearly fell through the floor, thirty feet to the ground.

My brother was understandably furious. Right up until that moment, I had been feeling like a real member of the team. My father and brother, along with a couple of other workers, were teaching me the ropes. The feeling of unity and camaraderie reminded me of my college basketball team. But I had failed in my job. I hadn't done what I was supposed to do. It was a powerful lesson for me that no matter how good the team, each of us is responsible to do our job.

No matter what the team, every day at work, every day of life at home and elsewhere, we are faced with one question: "Did you do your job?" Ideally, we should always be able to answer, "Yes, I did."

Ultimately, we can control only ourselves. What our intentions are, what we want our contribution to be, and even how alive and awake we want to feel each day—it's all up to us.

Joe and I were leading a discussion about teamwork for Kaiser

Permanente in California. The Kaiser executives were asking about improving the sense of individual accountability on their management teams. Joe got up and went to a chalkboard and started drawing X's in the shape of a football formation. The room turned silent, and everyone watched Joe.

"On an NFL team, everyone makes a difference," he said. He circled one of the eleven players. "Okay, let's say that during the course of a season, one guy regularly misses his assignment. The other ten guys can usually cover for him." He circled another player. "Now, two guys regularly miss their assignments—more than half the time you are going to lose." He circled a third player. "Now you're in last place. That is the level of personal accountability we relied on in the NFL. We knew it because we saw it, again and again, in our game films. Let me ask you, what are the stakes here at Kaiser if one individual does not perform at the required level?"

Remembering the "I" in "team" is not a selfish act. It is bigger than any of us alone; it's about us as individual members of a team. It's not "me" being self-centered and worried about my statistics; it is "I" as an individual centered in a place of personal responsibility, prepared to make that next level of commitment to the team.

Personal accountability is the foundation of the winning spirit.

Build Trust and Consideration

CONSIDERATION AND TRUST ARE KEY ELEMENTS TO BUILDING A WIN-ning team.

In sports and business, trust does not develop instantaneously. It takes time. We have to work every day on trust. It is not just a place that we can drop into now and then. Obviously, trust is established more quickly with some people than with others, but even with our best friends, we need to always maintain trust.

Being honest and having the proper attitude can help new teammates bypass months or even years of getting to know one another. Trust starts with someone promising to do something and then following through. It can be an individual experience, earning trust with another person, or a collective experience, building trust within the team.

Consideration, like trust, takes practice. Consideration enriches our relationships with family, friends, business associates, and teammates, as well as those casual relationships we have every day, such as at the store, post office, or dry cleaner. The practice of consideration is about valuing another human, putting ourselves in someone else's shoes, and seeing another perspective. It's about projecting kindness for others even when we don't know them, like them, or understand them.

A universal principle in recruiting outstanding team members is to seek individuals who display genuine consideration toward others. Of course, other traits and skills are also important in desirable team members, such as mental toughness, desire, focus, and confidence. But nothing is more important to overall morale and performance than having team members who are considerate of one another. With a roster of considerate players, a team is able to bond quickly and focus on achieving its goal.

A CEO of a large global corporation had to make a tough decision during difficult economic times: Let people go or reorganize the company. Realizing the importance of demonstrating company values through his own behavior, he chose to reduce his own salary over the course of three years; to significantly reduce expenditures; and to involve his employees in brainstorming solutions on how to cut expenses further. The company weathered the storm without having to lay off any workers. By positioning his employees to be part of the solution, the CEO showed not only high levels of trust and consideration, but that the company stood for empowerment and team spirit—not to mention profitability.

For someone to earn our trust, he or she should demonstrate a commitment to suiting up day after day without fail—at practice, in meetings, doing their mental and physical preparation—and showing up with energy and enthusiasm at crunch time. On the playing field or in a business setting, trust builds through consistency—of attendance, performance, and attitude.

Trust invites reciprocal trust. Truth inspires trust. Trust is, at its core, the choice to make oneself vulnerable, so when someone else is unafraid to show weakness, we are inclined to trust him or her with our own vulnerabilities. We open ourselves and let others in on our problems, concerns, and mistakes with the assurance that we will not be thought less of as a result.

A trusting relationship should be strong enough to allow forgiveness. We all fall short from time to time, act selfishly, or do something not up to our usual standards. If we are in a trusting relationship, we are already engaged in a cycle of giving and receiving. We forgive someone else for his or her mistakes, and we will be forgiven for our own. With this kind of understanding and generous interaction among team members, as we display our own trustworthiness, the trust others have in us will continue to grow.

Here is a story from Mitchell about trust building and one way to foster it within a team. "Every year in the preseason when I was a college basketball coach, I would bring my team to a ropes course for the guys to build their trust of one another and get to know each other better while being physically challenged. My assistant coaches and I did the course, too.

"One year, toward the end of a day of various trust-building and team-building activities, I was paired up with one of my players for an element called the Giant's Ladder. It looked like a giant ladder of telephone poles hanging in the air with cables on either side. The objective is to climb the giant ladder together. We were each in a safety harness, so if we fell, we would be caught. Our teammates were there with ropes to control our descent and keep us safe. We made it all the way to the top, fifty feet in the air, when my arms started giving out. Even though my head knew I was safely strapped in and I couldn't get hurt, my body didn't totally accept that notion. I hit the wall physically and lost my grip. I flipped over and found myself hanging upside down.

"My player's immediate reaction was to try and pull me back up, even though it would put him in jeopardy of slipping and falling over, too. Though helpless at that moment, I could see he was taking care of me. He had my back. I couldn't have uprighted myself without his help. Leveraging his body, he grabbed me and helped me to pull myself back up. As we reached the top of the pole together, everyone on the ground began to applaud. In challenging ourselves, we had learned a lot about being teammates.

"That player's name is Mark Georgi. It's no coincidence

that Mark became one of my all-time favorite players. In a moment when I was helpless, he was there for me without any hesitation. And he was a player that the team trusted tremendously, too. In pressure situations, we all could always count on Mark, who went on to win a four-year college basketball scholarship and later served as my assistant coach for five years.

"Rope courses are nothing new—they've been around for at least thirty years. My advice to anyone who has a team that is trying to bond and build trust: Find a ropes course and take your team. You won't regret it."

Montana

Trust binds winning teams together, whether in sports or in business. You want to trust how hard your teammates are going to work and how much they will try to do their job. That desire always made me want to show them how hard I would work and how much I cared about doing my job.

When I went into the financial investment business with Ronnie Lott and Harris Barton, we already trusted one another from football. Whenever we divided up the work that needed to be done, we knew the other guy was going to keep up his end, even if we went a week or longer without getting together. I suspect that's unusual with most start-ups, since trust is not immediate but something that needs to be earned. We were lucky.

As a quarterback, I trusted my blockers to block the defenders and keep them from getting to me before I could make a play. My blockers, in turn, trusted that if the opponents rushed me, I would try hard to get rid of the ball without taking a sack. (They hated sacks, as sacks given up are an important offensive-line statistic.) I trusted them not to make me look bad by having to spend the afternoon throwing under pressure, and they trusted me not to make them look bad by taking too many sacks.

I trusted John Taylor when he was supposed to run a twenty-yard pattern that he would not run eighteen yards, or twenty-four yards, but exactly twenty yards, which is where I would aim to deliver the ball in advance of his reaching the spot. If he wasn't where he was supposed to be, the pass would be incomplete or intercepted. Pass patterns start and end with trust between the quarterback and his receivers; they didn't want me throwing the ball up too high or putting it where they had to lay themselves out and be exposed to a crushing hit from a hard-charging defensive back.

Eleven teammates on the field at a time, all on an island together. If one of us made a mistake, we were all going to suffer. So we didn't kick a guy when he was down, because we knew we'd all be in his place sooner or later. We would find a way to cover for him, get him help with his blocking assignment or whatever it took, until he could get into the flow of things. That involved consideration, the twin of trust.

Through trust and consideration, we bonded together. I always made a deal with my center, who hiked me the ball on every play. I let him know that every time we messed up the exchange on the snap and the ball ended up on the ground, I would take the blame. I did so with the understanding that he would tell me what really happened, so we could work together to keep it from happening again. Anytime we had a bad snap, I went to the sidelines, shrugged, and told the coaches, "My fault."

Mitchell

Almost ten years ago, I spent a remarkable evening with UCLA coaching legend John Wooden at his home in Los Angeles. Coach Wooden's teams had won a record ten national basketball championships and went undefeated for four seasons, so I wanted to ask his advice on how to coach winning basketball. It soon became clear, however, that his true passion is discussing the intangible qualities that make true champions.

I took my assistant coaches with me, and they wanted answers to X-and-O questions about defensive and offensive sets. When Coach Wooden went into the other room to take a phone call from one of his former players, Bill Walton, I told the other coaches to please quit asking so many basketball questions because I wanted to talk with him about many other aspects of life.

When Coach Wooden came out, he delved right into the fun-

damentals of his famous "Pyramid of Success," which contains
building blocks such as Loyalty, Cooperation, Enthusiasm, Team
Spirit, and Poise.

I'll never forget the response I received when I asked, "Coach,
what was the one quality you looked for first and foremost when
recruiting a player?" I expected he might say something like mental toughness, competitive greatness, outstanding work ethic, un-
wavering dedication—all essential qualities for athletic success. But
his answer surprised me.

"Consideration for others. It is the essence of teamwork."

If he had not been a legend, I may have mistakenly thought
Coach Wooden's answer soft. But he had learned that in building
a team, the "soft stuff," like attitude and values, is much more difficult to find than the "hard stuff," like physical skills and natural
talent.

Coach Wooden did not invent the importance of being considerate to others or any of his other building blocks—they are all
universal principles—but he understood their importance and
used them extensively as a coach. He also made sure to embrace
them in his own life.

Coach Wooden was so generous with his time. We spent nearly
five hours in his company. We covered subjects as wide-ranging as
Kareem Abdul-Jabbar (Coach Wooden calls him Lewis), religion,
Abe Lincoln (a Coach Wooden favorite), racism in the old days,
winning ten national championships, family, the importance of
leadership, and what it means to be a man in this day and age.

When it was time to leave, I realized how genuinely moved I
had been by this man, then nearing his eighty-fifth birthday. He
gave me a lot of reading, including his classic basketball book, *Practical Modern Basketball,* and some poems he had written. As we
parted at the front door, I wanted to give him a hug, as you would
with your father or grandfather, but he gave me a firm handshake
and put his other hand on my forearm, as if to say, "No hugs."

My coaches and I walked to the car, along with our driver, a young man who worked for the UCLA athletic department. I felt deep emotion for this legendary coach. I had tears rolling down my cheeks. I was embarrassed and tried to wipe them away inconspicuously. "Don't worry about it," the driver said. "I often cry when I leave Coach Wooden."

The next day I sat on the edge of the bed, telling my wife, Adele, an artist and art teacher, about my amazing visit. All of a sudden, the tears came again. I was surprised. "What's this about, Adele?"

"Sounds like he's both a coach and a poet," she said. "Poetry and art bypass the rational mind and touch the soul. No wonder his players would go through walls for him."

Welcome Pressure

LEARNING TO PERFORM IN PRESSURE SITUATIONS IS OFTEN THE DIFFER-
ence between winning and losing in sports and in business. Those
who handle pressure best actually thrive on it when they perform.
They view pressure situations as challenges and opportunities.
Pressure performers have mastered the physical and mental skills
needed to execute, thus avoiding panic or loss of confidence at
crunch time, the definition of choking.

Some people do their best work under pressure. It helps them
block out everything other than the immediate goal. The ability to
play well under pressure is one of the most desired qualities for any
athlete in any sport, and the same holds true in the business environment, where an employee who succeeds under pressure is a
valued member of any team.

Performing well under pressure can be learned. First it is necessary to recognize that the pressure is created not by the game situation or a time deadline as much as it is by how we think and feel
about the particular situation. The difference between a football
game in midseason versus the Super Bowl is not the game itself but
the mental attitude and emotional intensity of the players, coaches,

staff, media, and even the fans. It's still two teams on a field trying to score the most points.

What makes outstanding performance under duress possible is the ability to concentrate on the task at hand rather than reacting to the tension and emotion of the situation—time remaining on the clock, the score, people yelling in the stands. Inability to control our emotions or our thoughts results in a lack of concentration. We get anxious or nervous and tighten up. A great performer concentrating on his or her job will be much too engaged to think about anything other than what is happening in that moment.

Some athletes have developed techniques to help them relax in pressure situations. A former top relief pitcher used to step off the mound for a few moments and think of fishing in a favorite lake high in the Colorado mountains. The sense of tranquillity and peace it brought helped calm his mind and relax his body. He went so far as to imagine the call of birds overhead and the buzz of insects. Then he took a few deep breaths, stepped back on the mound, and pitched.

Relaxation, poise, and concentration can all be learned, as with any other skill. Performing under pressure is a developed habit. By practicing and perfecting during real-life situations, as well as simulated ones in disciplined practices, we can learn how to block out distractions and concentrate on those basic, fundamental skills.

In addition to physically working on pressure situations in practice, learning to control our thinking is also helpful. We should practice replacing unproductive thoughts, which lead to fear and worry and doubt, with productive thoughts, which help us relax, stay focused, execute with intelligence, and perform with confidence. This type of mental training is necessary to give us an advantage—an edge—in pressure situations. We want to be free of negative thoughts in order to see clearly what we need to do.

Under pressure, we train ourselves to exercise good judgment and have control of our skills, thoughts, and emotions.

Whether you're a professional athlete playing in a championship game or an accountant working to meet a tax deadline, demonstrating grace and poise under fire will help you stay focused and do your job better.

PRACTICE: The night before your next big performance in sports or business, go into a room where you can be alone. Get into a comfortable position and practice a few minutes of relaxation. In your mind, see yourself where you will be performing. As you think about what you have to accomplish, you may begin to feel some anxiety. That's good! Invite and welcome all the tension you can feel. As the intensity within you begins to build, breathe deeply. Continue your deep breathing and see yourself exactly how you wish to perform, at your very best—whether it's scoring the winning points or making an important speech. This creates a mental picture of success. Continue to let the pressure and intensity grow. Keep breathing deeply. Welcome that pressure and intensity.

Montana

When the 49ers were in a pressure situation, such as on the short end of the score late in the game, we went back to the basics. We ran plays that we had been running since the first day of training camp and knew better than any others. It wasn't about tricking anyone; it was about execution. We knew if we performed the way we were capable of performing and had done so often in practice, we would succeed.

Two minutes is a lot of time in a football game. Even a minute and thirty seconds with two time-outs can be an eternity. In most any pressure situation, I always thought we had plenty of time. Plenty of time to score, as long as we kept our cool. The average pass play takes six or seven seconds. If we kept moving the ball, even only five yards at a time, we'd eventually get into the end zone. I never felt rushed, though I did realize there was no room for mistakes. No interceptions or fumbles. If a pass was incomplete, the clock stopped, which gave us more time to think about what to do next.

A lot of athletes talk about being in the zone during pressure situations. For me, being in the zone means a higher state of concentration. When we let our mind wander, we make mistakes. When we start thinking about bad things that have happened or good things that could happen, our focus is not where it should be—on this play, right here, right now.

Staying cool isn't easy. We have to work at it and practice it, like anything else. I get nervous and scared, too. In the 1981 NFC championship game against the Dallas Cowboys, I threw my third interception late in the fourth quarter, with the Cowboys up 27–21. All the fans of "The Catch" probably don't remember that, only that we won the game in the final seconds of play. If a fellow doesn't get nervous in a situation like that, he isn't breathing. At those times it's important to keep your mind *off* the mistakes and *on* your goal.

At some point in my career, I came to welcome pressure situations, because I knew they would test me and my team to see what we were made of, and I felt we were up to the challenge. These are opportunities to develop more confidence, trust, and mental toughness. Plus, it's a lot more fun to win a close one against a worthy opponent than to trounce a mediocre team.

Not long ago, I visited my alma mater, Notre Dame, and talked to the football team. Some of the players began to complain about the difficulty of their schedule, since they would be playing some top-ranked football teams that season. "Why did you come here to an excellent school with a reputation for great football?" I asked. "Why didn't you go to a school with less of a reputation and less expectation of playing winning football? I assume all of you chose to come here because you want the best, and you want to play against the best. And that your desire is so great and so strong that you will strive with all your might to find ways to win. Facing top teams is the only way you will improve your own game. Welcome the competition."

The best competitors always want to be around the best. Pressure situations test us and our team to see what we are made of.

Some competitors make the mistake of having interim goals. We should be clear about what it is we want to accomplish, and not take any of the pressure off ourselves until we reach it. I've seen NFL teams and coaches relax when they win their division—maybe everyone figured their jobs were safe for another year—and then fail to advance in the championship series. If the goal is to win the division, fine. But if it's to go all the way and win the Super Bowl, which it should be, then everyone needs to stay focused until they've done it.

For the same reason, I never paid attention during the season to incentive clauses in my contracts. These clauses paid a player more money based on statistics. All of my contracts had them, and I was glad they did, but I never thought about them during the season. If the incentive was for me to throw thirty TDs to receive a bonus, and I reached that by the tenth game and thought about it, I might assume my season was over. But there were more games to be played, and a championship to win.

When it came to playing under pressure, there were times when I was nervous, although I was always less nervous in the game than when waiting to go in. (And I'm a *lot* more nervous today, watching my children play sports, than I ever was when I played.) While I might have looked cool on the outside, inside I could get upset like anyone else. But I tried not to let my nerves overtake my mental state or my ability to function. I didn't fear being in the game, playing quarterback, making split-second decisions. I craved it.

Mitchell

A lot of college football fans noticed early in Joe's career that he excelled in pressure situations and could engineer come-from-behind heroics with what most of us would consider very little time left on the clock. Joe always felt that a scant few minutes—a deadline most of us would find daunting—seemed abundant to him and his team to do what they had to do to win.

If those last-minute victories had happened only a few times, they might have been remembered as unique highlights in his career. But he became a legend at Notre Dame—known as "Joe Cool" and "The Comeback Kid"—because he routinely pulled off last-minute heroics with his passes, scrambling, field presence, and intelligence. Joe's ability to excel under pressure followed him to the NFL, where he engineered thirty-one fourth-quarter comebacks in his career.

Handling pressure with poise and confidence, while believing victory is inevitable, is a fascinating example of the winning spirit.

Obviously, someone in Joe's position needed to have the physical ability to mount the comeback charge, but when someone does it so frequently that it becomes a trademark, we should take the opportunity to dive into the psyche of that person and ask: "How?"

When Joe gets into any kind of situation where there is pressure to perform, he drops back into a zone of clarity and groundedness. He tells me it's not as if things slow down for him; rather, he's overcome with a sense that there is enough time to do what he needs to do. He doesn't just *say* this to himself; it's something he feels in his bones. It is a state of hope and belief in himself. It is a state of extreme optimism.

We all love having individuals on our team who thrive on pressure. So many things in sports and business come down to the wire—the pressure of a deadline, bettering the competition—that having someone on your team who has learned how to use pressure to his or her advantage is a real plus.

Competition and pressure bring out feelings of anxiety in most of us, because we know we are expected to be at our best. Often we are being watched, judged, and evaluated in some form or another. Competition forces us into the spotlight, often alone, even when a member of a team. Expectations from others—coaches, supervisors, parents, friends, teammates—make us feel all the more anxious. If we strive for performance excellence, we must perform regularly under all sorts of pressure, as Joe did, only probably not with the Cotton Bowl or Super Bowl on the line. We will be under the critical eyes of others, not only teammates but competitors, and there will often be something at stake.

Since pressure and tension are unavoidable in a big, well-lived life, why not welcome them? Instead of struggling against it, we should embrace the pressure we feel and let it help us be even better. We should thrive on the energy it gives us. When we find ourselves in an intense pressure situation, we want to believe we can win and say, "I *love* the pressure. Bring it on!"

PART THREE

Keep the Winning Spirit Alive

Keep the Winning Spirit Alive

THE PRACTICE AND APPLICATION OF TIME-TESTED PRINCIPLES FOR PERformance excellence keep the winning spirit alive. All of us can attend a workshop, read a book, listen to a tape, or otherwise be temporarily inspired, then forget most of what we learned. Applying and practicing the principles daily will anchor our learning and deepen those lessons.

The five principles in this section offer more ways to implement winning behaviors and habits into our everyday lives. The winning spirit doesn't show up just in big games or during a championship run but in simple daily actions, too. Success is built on small wins as well as big ones.

There will be days when it is difficult to muster enough energy to be our best. We may be tired or frustrated or in a bad mood. There may be unforeseen circumstances and distractions, setbacks and injuries. Professional or personal issues may arise. Nevertheless, these are the times when it is most important to push onward and stay focused. We do not want to give in to a belief that we are victims of circumstance. Even in our darkest hours and toughest challenges, we must give it everything we have if we wish to succeed.

The winning spirit is kept alive by living and performing in the moment, visualizing success, finding the support of a coach and inner circle, making a personal commitment to excellence, living a disciplined life, affirming our truest values—all while believing in our ability to achieve our goal.

PRINCIPLE #12

Perform in the Moment

GREAT PERFORMANCES OCCUR IN THE PRESENT, NOT IN THE PAST OR future.

Although recalling positive memories of past performances and visualizing future ones can be useful, the best state of mind to be in is the present. When we focus our attention into the present, we emit a field of energy that translates into power and command. We project calmness, poise, and confidence. We become aware of what is happening and what we need to do.

As basic as it sounds, the principle of being in the moment is not taught in schools or at work, although some college and professional sports teams espouse it. Some disciplines such as yoga, meditation, and relaxation training help. When we were young, we all knew how to live in the moment. Should you ever forget, watch young children playing. You see young bodies and minds fully engaged in the here and now, not concerned with yesterday or tomorrow.

Living in the present moment can be relearned and practiced daily. Relaxed concentration is crucial to living in the moment. Staying in an aware yet relaxed state of mind gives us the mental, emotional, and physical focus to allow things to flow naturally, so we can become immersed in the here and now.

Living in the present allows us to relax under pressure. The chances of a terrific performance increase for an individual or team maintaining relaxed, moment-to-moment focus during a pressure situation. Most coaches and players know this to be true, even though not enough teams consciously practice the art.

The Chicago Bulls, during their record-breaking championship run, were an exception. Bulls coach Phil Jackson hired a mindfulness coach, George Mumford, to work with his players. Jackson and Mumford had both studied Eastern philosophies and practiced meditation for twenty-five years. Essentially, Mumford taught the Bulls a meditation practice to help them stay in the moment.

He took the Bulls through their paces on game days, asking them to concentrate on their breathing, individually and together; Mumford referred to the latter as "conspiring together." The group breathed together to achieve team unity—having the same intention, goal, and purpose. Individually, they breathed to relax into the feeling of confidence and readiness, to increase energy for better performance, and to free the mind of worry, fear, and tension.

During these sessions, often conducted on the floor of a hotel conference room, Mumford gave the players keys to use in a game when they needed to calm their thoughts and redirect their energies. The referee's whistle, for example, was one good time to take inventory; when a player stepped to the free-throw line was another. Find the time, he counseled, to live fully in the moment.

Mumford, who also worked with the L.A. Lakers when Phil Jackson was coach, currently works with sports teams at Boston College. He still remembers his best student on the Bulls, none other than Michael Jordan. "Michael made no distinction between practice and a game in terms of the effort he put in," Mumford recalled. "He was the first one running sprints and doing all the other drills. He didn't have to prove anything, and yet he was always pushing himself. Not in an abusive way, but because he was truly in the moment and enjoying what he was doing."

Jordan once described to Mumford what happened for him during a game. All the other players were moving in slow motion, but Jordan felt that his body was moving even slower. He felt as if he had all the time in the world to make a shot or move to the basket. He believed this also allowed him to anticipate where other players were going, and enabled him to get there before they did.

Studies have been done with athletes about what happens when they are in the zone, when events seem to slow down and perception becomes more vivid. The senses become keen and awake, and the mind becomes focused and clear. Being in the zone is when human potential is best realized, and the peak performer is deeply engaged in the moment.

Before, during, and after practice and competition, constantly remind yourself, "Right here is the best place, and right now is the only time."

PRACTICE: Set aside ten minutes to allow yourself to drop fully and deeply into the moment. Find a comfortable chair where you can sit with a straight back. Place your hands on your knees and close your eyes. Begin to pay attention to your breathing. Don't force or change anything. Just notice your breath flowing in and out of your body. Notice the ease of your breathing. Breathe in. Breathe out. Breathe in. Breathe out. When you find that your mind has wandered off and you catch yourself thinking about other things, simply bring your full attention back to your breathing. In this exercise, there is no goal to achieve, nothing to win, but an opportunity in the day to more fully drop into the present moment. It can be both relaxing and exhilarating.

Montana

Sports are excellent training for being in the moment.

Football, basketball, soccer, equestrian events—it's nearly impossible to be involved in competition without being fully present. It goes back, I think, to sports being a game meant to be played for fun. How often does the mind wander when we're playing and having fun? If you're like me, not often.

In football, no matter how long the road back was—even when we were down with time running out—I never wanted to look too far off. I always wanted to stay in the present. Especially when you're behind, the goal is to execute successfully, but you don't have to do everything all at once. You want to stay inside yourself and get a flow going. Little pieces of progress are the key to winning. Only when you feel comfortable do you want to take a bigger chance or two and go for it.

Anytime I found myself worrying too far down the line or into the future, I knew I was wasting energy. It was more important to take that shorter look at the field and the game. I'd remind myself, "Right here. Right now."

Likewise, whenever I found myself thinking about past mistakes and wishing I could have another chance, I'd pull myself back. If my mind wasn't in the present moment, the here and now, my body and energy wouldn't be, either. The present was something I could control, unlike those useless thoughts about a past or future situation that wasn't in my control at all.

It's the same regardless of one's game or occupation—a golfer missing a putt, a shortstop letting the ball go through his legs, a salesman making a pitch but not getting the sale. There will be another putt soon, and another grounder for the shortstop, and another opportunity to make a sale. If we are so shaken by the past that we can't stay right here and now, paying attention to what needs to be done, we will not execute to the best of our ability.

With the 49ers, one thing that helped keep everyone present was the way, come Monday, we threw out everything we had studied for the previous week. After the game was over on Sunday, that was it. We had to prepare anew, and we went into that period of study with a beginner's mind-set. The coaches would put in new defenses, new blitzes, new pass plays, and lots of other new wrinkles we all needed to know and practice. Additionally, we were kept way too busy, physically and mentally, to find the time or desire to look two or three games down the road. One game at a time was plenty.

Sometimes the game at hand had nothing to do with the real game. Before our regular practice sessions, different position players would get together for specialty practice. The other quarterbacks and I soon came up with our own drill: to see how many rolls of tape each of us could throw into the hollow top of a ten-foot-high portable goalpost. We became quite competitive. When the whistle blew for practice, I'd often lag behind a couple of minutes, trying hard to sink my last few rolls of tape into that darn pipe. Anyone who noticed what I was doing probably saw in me a guy who looked about as determined to win this little game as I would be to win the big one come Sunday.

Whether I'm playing a silly game of "sink the tape in the pipe" or practicing or competing, I always try to have fun and stay fully committed and focused in the present moment. There's really no place else I would rather be.

Mitchell

When athletes first start a sport, they want to learn as much as possible. Open-minded, enthusiastic, and willing to be taught, they practice and compete with childlike exuberance. They have the mentality of a beginner. Over time, things can change. Their minds mature and close. Learning and improving—and enjoying the present—stop.

One reason that athletes lose their childlike enthusiasm for the game is that it becomes a business. Whether it's the international track-and-field circuit or the World Series, winning and getting paid big dollars become huge factors in competitive life. Athletes sometimes lose touch with whatever drew them to their sport in the first place. Some may even begin to take their natural athletic abilities and hard-earned skills for granted, and as they do, their passion starts to fade.

Chris Mullin, who is now vice president of the Golden State Warriors, told me that when he evaluates players, he looks not only at how their skills, athletic ability, and personality would fit on the team, but also at their level of love for the game. "I want guys who would play even if they didn't get paid for it."

Certainly, Mullin fell into that category as a player. Not long after we first met, Mullin and I played a two-on-two pickup game at a local gym against Rod Higgins and Brent Barry, former and current NBA players, respectively. It was my first time playing with Mully. After the game, as we drove back to his house, I told Mully I was looking forward to seeing him play next season.

He gave me a disappointed look. "What do you think we just did?"

"I mean a real game."

"That was for real, Tom. Do you think I play any different with my friends than I do in front of twenty thousand people? It's the same game for me. Playing basketball *anywhere* is what I love to do."

I eventually learned something else about Mullin—whenever he stepped to the free-throw line, he had taught himself to empty his mind. He dropped all thought and let his body, mechanics, and training take over. It was a facet of his individual preparation, yes, but it was also a classic example of being present in the moment. And a successful one, given that Mully finished his career with an impressive 87 percent free-throw percentage.

When we live in the moment, we go back to playing for the love of the game before we had any other reasons to do so. Our mind is open, and our enthusiasm is contagious. We want to improve, and we want to be taught. We look forward to practice as well as competitive situations.

Collegiate stars, Olympians, and professionals: At some point they all need to find ways to reawaken their innocence and child-like enthusiasm and to regain a beginner's mentality without losing the competitive edge.

None of us can live or perform too much in the here and now. The more we can train ourselves, talk to ourselves, and teach ourselves to be in the moment—to live for today—the happier and more successful we will be.

When I'm coaching executives, being present is a topic that frequently comes up for discussion. Financial pressures, deadlines, and personal distractions can make it difficult to stay present and not become preoccupied. Together with clients, we create a customized plan that helps them practice living in the present moment. Again, it is not a formula that can be passed from one person to the next; rather, it must fit individual needs and beliefs.

It can be as simple as learning breath control or practicing becoming a conscious and active listener, perhaps for the first fifteen minutes after you've come home from work and a family member wants to tell you about his or her day. We can also allocate a part of each day to doing one thing and one thing only. Not eating and watching TV, for example, but really enjoying one or the other. Not talking on the cell phone while playing a game at the beach with the kids, but enjoying the sun, the waves, their peals of laughter—the moment.

One executive has taken this practice to heart and has found a unique way to remember the power of now. He starts each morning by placing a smooth pebble (touchstone) in one pocket. Anytime throughout the day after he has been fully present and deeply listened to another person, he switches the pebble to the other pocket. The switch may occur after he listens to a concern, gives some needed information, or offers genuine words of encouragement. This exercise is a simple but effective way to remember the importance of being present.

I will always remember something else about my five-hour visit with UCLA's Coach Wooden—something that went to the heart of living in the moment. He told me when I am coaching a team not to spend too much time talking to the players about the outcome—namely, winning.

"Don't coach and teach too much about where you want to be," Coach Wooden said. "Coach and teach about where you are as a team right now, and what you want to do right now in order to play your best."

Visualize Success

VISUALIZATION IS AN EFFECTIVE MENTAL TOOL FOR OBTAINING POSITIVE results.

There are three crucial aspects to successful visualization: concentration, imagination, and repetition. By concentrating on the image or outcome we desire, we can step into an "as if" reality, experiencing something as if it is really happening.

As we hold this image in our mind's eye and imagine it as our reality, we have begun the process of what is called "creative manifestation." When practiced properly, confidence and trust that our dream will come true increase. We set the energy in motion, and at least in our inner world, we have experienced it as real.

An important aspect of this visualization process is imagination. We must be able to imagine what it is we desire to create. The more detail, the better. If we can clearly imagine the event or feel the outcome that we strive for, the visualization process will be easier and more effective.

In the classic movie *It's a Wonderful Life,* a small-town banker is allowed to see the kind of miserable world he would create for himself and others should he make a terrible choice, and he climbs back into the present to make the best choice—"a wonderful life." Through visualization we strive to do that in reverse. We want to see and feel the wonderful life in front of us, knowing that it is ours for the making but that we'll have to choose well along the way to achieve it.

One of the best things about the practice of visualization is that we can do it anytime, anywhere, and on our own. We can do it in the quiet of our bedroom or prior to an event, a performance, or a game. We can even practice it in the midst of a performance or competition. A former world-class marathon runner, whenever he came to a hill, visualized a powerful magnet pulling him effortlessly to the top. Before every speech, a successful motivational speaker sees her audience excited and engaged in her message. She even imagines the thunderous applause of the audience.

As we develop new goals and aspirations, our visualization process can be the secret to our success each and every time. However, it is important to remember that in visualizing our success, repetition is key. When practicing visualization, we should incorporate breathing and relaxation techniques. Also, a few attempts are not usually enough to enjoy the benefits of visualization. Our minds need repetition to integrate the image into our bodies. The more we practice visualization, the more we build and create momentum toward our goal.

Athletes are not alone in achieving results through visualization. It can also be effective in the business community, when used as a way to accelerate one's ability to realize results. The same visualization techniques apply in business: Concentrate on what you want to create, vividly imagine yourself doing it, and rehearse it over and over. Executives are coached to visualize the outcome of an event—a staff meeting, a public speech, the launch of a new product, exceeding a sales goal—as a tool to boost their preparation. The idea is to imagine it until you feel as if you've done it all the time: "See it, believe it, achieve it."

Everyone knows the feeling of awakening from a dream and thinking how real it felt. Visualization can feel just as real. We want to engage the aspect of our brain that creates pathways and patterns, in order to accomplish exactly what we want. Through regular visualization, we will be able to create a bridge from where we are to where we want to be.

Added benefits from the practice of visualization include: improved commitment to practice with energy, increased confidence in our ability to perform under pressure, greater ability to retain information, and a more positive self-image.

During the Vietnam War, an American POW who endured several years of captivity helped keep his sanity by mentally playing his favorite golf course over and over again. For eighteen holes, he visualized each and every shot, where the ball ended up, which club to use next, and so on. After every game, he pictured cleaning his clubs and putting them away with his golf shoes. When he was released, he went to that golf course. He played eighteen holes and, much to his surprise, dropped ten strokes off his previous best score—without having picked up a club in years.

One way to enhance the power of visualization is to affirm what you are envisioning in a short, simple statement. Verbally state or write down that which you envision yourself doing. During this process, acknowledge the outcome you desire. Such as: "I am powerfully leading my team to great success." Repeat this affirmation often—silently or aloud—throughout the day. Write it out and place it at several locations where you can see it regularly: on your computer, in your calendar or PDA, at the office, in the car. The more you integrate your words with your images, the better. Experiment and try different words and combinations until you find something unique and meaningful.

Although the use of words and mental pictures helps us to achieve the success we desire, we must still give the experience emotion and feeling. Remember, our emotions are the passion and driving force behind everything we do. By bringing it all together—our visualizations, affirmations, the power of our passion—we propel ourselves toward the results we wish to achieve with new enthusiasm and belief.

PRACTICE: Identify one area in your life—finances, relationships, career, parenting—in which you want certain positive changes and results. Close your eyes, take a deep breath, relax your body, clear your mind, and identify the specific goal or result you want to accomplish. Become clear about the result, experience, or reward that you want to achieve. Now imagine yourself sometime in the future, having already accomplished your goal. See yourself living your dream, and bring all your senses into the pictures—sights, scents, sounds, textures, and emotions. Who is in the picture with you? What are you saying? What are you doing? How does it feel?

Montana

The main reason Bill Walsh used to diagram the first twenty-five plays of the game and hand them out to us ahead of time was so we could picture exactly what it was we wanted to accomplish. Now, it's true that what we envisioned didn't always happen, but a good percentage of the time, it did.

In visualizing a number of plays into the game, some of the guys had something to look forward to—getting the ball on a particular run play, or being the primary receiver for a pass. They could start thinking ahead about how they would run, and cut, and the moves they would make once the ball was in their hands.

Sometimes we had to deviate from the script. If we got backed up against our end zone or moved the ball down to within striking distance of the opponent's end zone, Coach Walsh would call in different plays. But most of the time, the offensive unit started down the field knowing exactly what would come next.

A game plan could be mastered only by studying the playbook. After I had all the terminology down, I would take each play and trace over it in my playbook with a red felt pen. I would do this each night during the week, usually four or five times before the game on Sunday.

After tracing and retracing the plays, I would close my eyes and visualize what would happen once the ball was snapped. I saw where the players would be lined up for each play. I visualized the pass patterns that would be run by four or five receivers. I would see the linemen in front of me, then concentrate on where the receivers were instructed to end up, where I would deliver the ball ahead of their arrival. When a play was called in a game—"Red Left Slot Waggle Right X Out"—the entire picture snapped to mind.

Watching films also helped us visualize. When it was footage of us, we could see exactly what we had done wrong and learn from it so we didn't repeat the same mistake. When it was film of our upcoming opponent, we could envision how to get an advantage.

Visualization is an important part of mental preparation. I have used it a lot since I left the game: seeing what I want and expect to happen in business, for example, as with all those plays I used to commit to memory.

For five years, Jennifer and I looked for property to build our home on. We could each see it and describe it in detail, but nothing the Realtors showed us looked like it. The vision of what we wanted was so clear to us that we knew it had to exist. Eventually, we did find it and build our home. If we hadn't had that vision, we would have settled for something else and always wondered if we had missed out on our dream.

Most people visualize with their eyes closed, but when you get good enough at it, you can do it with your eyes open. Visualizing specifically and realistically what we see ourselves doing can help us move into a confident and relaxed state so that we are better able to execute.

I've done it with football plays, business deals, and that dream property. It's not fantasizing. It's more like rehearsing. As they said in *Caddyshack,* a favorite movie of mine: "See your future, be your future."

Mitchell

At one point in my college basketball coaching career, we were in a sixteen-team tournament in which we had finished second the year before. After beating three other teams, we were back in the championship game for the second year in a row. Shortly before game time, I found myself slipping back into an old way of thinking. I began obsessing over our need to win this championship game.

All year I had been preaching to my team to focus on the things within our control and not to worry so much about the final outcome. I wanted us to do everything to be a great team: Play with heart. Be tough. Execute. Talk to each other when playing defense. Be unselfish.

But that day I couldn't shake my thinking about the year before. I feared losing the championship game—again. I thought, I am going to face this fear head-on. I went into the training room by myself and stretched out on the table. Closing my eyes, I visualized the game we were about to play. I went through everything—my guys playing hard, close calls, offensive and defensive sets, and then, in the end, us losing again. I even saw myself shaking the hand of the winning coach and experiencing the feelings of disappointment and failure as I walked off the court.

I took a few deep breaths, then realized that I still had my job, I still loved my players for trying so hard, and I knew that I was still a good coach. It wasn't the end of the world. We didn't have to win the trophy to be a great team. Sure, it would be nice, but there was much more to it than taking home the trophy.

I got up, went into the locker room, and addressed my team. I reminded them how far we had come to get here and thanked them for their hard work. We went out, and they played great. Throughout the game, I coached from a place of calmness and confidence, because I wasn't so afraid of losing. And guess what happened? We won the game and the championship. Although most of the time we want to visualize the exact outcome we desire, my exercise worked because it allowed me to face my fear of failure.

When I interview NBA players for pre-draft evaluations, I ask what led them to professional basketball. They almost always tell me they've dreamed of being in the NBA since childhood. They've visualized the court, the crowds, the other players, even the team uniform. It's true that a lot of young players have similar dreams that never come true, but I think the success of those who make their dreams come true has a lot to do with visualization.

Brian Boitano, one of the greatest men's ice-skating champions and the 1988 Olympic gold medal winner, told me how he used visualization to aid his performances. He practiced his program over and over mentally, visualizing every move and jump until he could do them perfectly in his mind. He then tried to duplicate that perfection on the ice. Before the Olympics, he went so far as to visualize the awards ceremony where he would receive the gold medal. He even imagined hearing the national anthem.

We can visualize from now until doomsday, but not many of us will be professional athletes or Olympic champions. Visualization is not a substitute for ability. I've heard Joe Montana deliver the same message. The question is not whether we can be as good as Brian Boitano or Michael Jordan or Joe Montana, but rather: "Do you want to be as good as you can possibly be?"

When I'm working with college athletes who want to become professional athletes, or high school athletes who want to play Division I college sports, I discuss with them all the steps and actions that they will need to take to get there. Their physical conditioning, skill development, attitude—everything necessary to get them from point A to point B. Then I ask them to imagine that they have already arrived at their destination. They've become the pro athlete or Division I player that they strive to be—what is it they think they'll feel like when they are there? What will the uniform look like? What kind of money will they make in the pros? I want them to begin to experience what pride and success will feel like. It's kind of like time-traveling. I'm asking them to go from here to there, experience the feeling, then bring it back with them to now, so that in this moment, at this time, they can feel success and feel pride.

Walt Whitman said a hundred years ago, "Henceforth I ask not good-fortune, I myself am good-fortune." To become now, in our minds, that which we seek in the future is an effective way to look at preparation for anything in life. Free your mind, and your body will follow.

Find a Coach and an Inner Circle

MOST PEAK PERFORMERS RECEIVE SOME TYPE OF COACHING. KNOWING to ask for help is a major step in personal growth. Seeking another point of view from someone we trust and respect is often exactly what is needed to reach the next level.

Without the accumulated knowledge imparted by coaches and mentors through simple, direct instructions, learning new skills or improving old ones can be difficult. It is also important that we communicate back to them. Expressing our emotions and letting a coach or mentor know what is going on inside our head is crucial. We cannot assume that they know what we are thinking or understand everything we are going through.

A coach becomes a member of our inner circle, a valuable support group made up of those people who have our best interests at heart, such as parents, family, and true friends. These are the people we want to listen to carefully because we can trust them, and we should place value on their opinions, comments, and observations.

There will be those in our orbit at work and elsewhere who will comment on our abilities and performances. Remember that these individuals are not members of our inner circle. They may sometimes say kind things and at other times make unkind comments. They may not have our best interests at heart. It can be difficult to let negative comments roll off your back, but that is what you must do in order to be free of them.

Receiving trustworthy feedback is invaluable for anyone wishing to improve his or her performance. Being the best at something includes learning from others, modeling our behavior after them, and stretching ourselves beyond what we thought possible. A coach will accelerate the process.

Coaching is an industry that is no longer only specialized for athletes or elite clients. Now, most people can find, hire, and work with a coach. We may want to do so in any number of ways. We might use a coach when we're going through a career transition, trying to get in shape, reconnecting with or refining our purpose in life, enhancing parenting skills, developing creativity, improving self-esteem, or wanting to deepen a love relationship.

In business, a coach can help us work not only harder but smarter, and find ways to achieve better results with ease. The most successful coaches are those who learn how to build up and maintain someone's self-confidence while assisting in other areas, such as goal-setting, motivation, dealing with mistakes, handling criticism, and boosting communication skills. A coach is an invaluable resource recognized by many large and small companies as a necessity to help a staff improve performance. Companies such as IBM, Motorola, J. P. Morgan Chase, and Hewlett-Packard all employ coaches for their managers and up-and-comers. According to a recent survey, between 25 and 40 percent of Fortune 500 companies use executive coaches. These companies are giving their valued employees and best prospects what star athletes have long had: a trusted adviser to help them improve their performance and reach their goals.

"Many of us at my company were so busy," explained a computer-company executive, "that we were channeling our energy into doing what was urgent. We lost sight of our long-term goals. The value of working with a coach who you respect and trust is impossible to overestimate. An unbiased, nonjudgmental coach provides new direction, support, and a safe sounding board."

There are several practical ways to evaluate whether someone is worth pursuing as a potential coach, mentor, or member of our inner circle. Do we trust the direction the coach is taking us? Do we feel confident in her expertise? Is it easy to be honest around him? Does she have the ability to bring out the best in me and my team? Choose coaches, mentors, and supporters carefully. Observe them working, and ask smart questions.

A coach is someone who sees what we cannot always see in our own lives. He collaborates with us, challenges us, and tells us the truth as he sees it. An extraordinary coach helps us to clarify our values and to design a life honoring them. A coach assists us in crystallizing our thoughts by asking probing and thought-provoking questions. A coach sometimes expects more from us than we expect of ourselves, and can often shift us out of our comfort zone.

We become a coach's dream by working hard, listening, and wanting to improve. We make no excuses for what happened yesterday but give our full focus to today's challenges. We put all our heart and mind into the task at hand. We understand the meaning of commitment. When different situations arise, we are tough and courageous. We know there is no challenge too big for us to handle, because we have the strength and desire necessary to reach our goals.

PRACTICE: Remember a coach, teacher, supervisor, mentor, or anyone else who's had positional authority in your life. He or she should be someone you idealized and thought had the qualities that went into being a positive role model. If you are still able to get in touch with that person, ask him or her to be frank with you: "Tell me about me." Find out what kind of player or client you were. What kind of teammate? Were you a coach's dream? Find out the truth and learn from it.

Montana

When I speak at motivational seminars, I like to leave the audience with this message: "If you're really committed to excellence in any field, find a performance coach who can help guide you to a higher level of achievement. Whether it's a trainer at the gym, a mentor at the office, or an instructor to improve your golf game, that's how we get better."

Sometimes the most gifted performers don't make the best coaches. The best violinist in the orchestra would not necessarily make a skilled teacher or even conductor. I know I wouldn't make a very good coach because I don't have the patience, and I'd expect everyone to work as hard as, well—Ronnie Lott, Jerry Rice, and the rest of the guys. Not likely to happen.

So, when it comes to picking a coach, select wisely.

Sometimes we get lucky and join a team that happens to have a good coach already in place. Someone like Bill Walsh. He drafted me, and I ended up learning from the most innovative football coach in history. I learned a lot from Coach Walsh throughout my career, but the one thing that has stuck is a desire to be perfect. He pushed me and pushed us—especially the quarterback position, which he was so proud of—to seek perfection. If you miss perfection, you end up with greatness, and he could handle that but nothing less.

There was something else I learned from Coach Walsh. My first year, I got a little carried away and signed a number of endorsement deals. My face was out before the public quite a bit, considering how little I was playing. Bill came up to me one day and said, "Joe, the less people see you, the more they want you." No truer words were ever spoken.

My first coach in life was pretty wise, too. My dad was the first to teach me the importance of practicing not just for the best-case scenario but for the worst possible situation. I have since discovered this works in many aspects of life. Something about always being prepared is the way my dad put it.

One day at a basketball court near our house, my dad found me practicing my right-handed jumper. "What are you doing?" he asked.

"Practicing my shot." I was standing in my favorite spot making one after the other.

"That's not practicing," he said. "You think in a game they're gonna let you stand in your favorite spot and shoot away?"

He showed me what he had in mind. He'd played basketball in the navy, and it was his best sport. We went one-on-one. He grabbed me, he pushed me, he threw his elbows at me. I kept saying, "Dad, you can't do that," but he kept it up. If I tried to go up for a rebound, he'd step on my foot; if I started to go around him, he'd trip me as I went by. He taught me how to shoot all over the court, and with my left hand. We practiced over and over all those things that you don't expect to happen in a game. I learned his tricks and how to avoid them. As I got quicker, I could get around him no matter what he did. Eventually, there was no dirty trick an opponent could do to me that my father hadn't done a hundred times before.

In my inner circle, there were some pretty special people who watched out for my best interests. Folks like Mike DeCicco, the Notre Dame football team's academic adviser—he also made sure we got to classes on time and didn't cut any. Unfortunately, I had his mimeographed note memorized: *Please report to Mr. DeCicco's office immediately. No excuses will be accepted.* He became my surrogate father, and his wife, Paulie, my surrogate mother, during my first time away from home. They took me into their house and treated me like family. I have thanked them before, but words alone somehow aren't enough.

My success in and out of football would not have been possible without those people who believed in me, and my coaches and mentors who generously taught me what they knew. An inner circle should be made up of people whom we trust with our truest thoughts and feelings. Since they will so often be keepers of our confidences, and have our back in difficult times, we want them to be loyal and trustworthy. We must choose wisely.

Mitchell

Capturing the winning spirit is not a solo enterprise.

While we will be accountable for our own efforts, our dreams most likely will involve others: teammates, colleagues at work, family, friends. We want to be clear about who cares the most for us, and who has membership in our inner circle. Once we identify them, we should frequently acknowledge what they mean to us. Without them, our chances of success diminish. We may also want to ask ourselves whose inner circle we are part of. Living with the winning spirit includes the cycle of giving and receiving.

People find coaches to work with in a variety of ways. My own opportunity to become a performance coach came from an unusual situation. When I was still coaching basketball, my team lost a close game one night. One of our players missed a game-winning layup in the final seconds. The young man felt responsible for the loss. He was in tears. I called in his teammates, and we rallied around the player, letting him know everything was okay and that we still believed in him.

Later, as we headed to the locker room, a college friend, John Polumbo, who had come to watch my team play, approached me. John was then vice president of a national telecommunications company. He told me he was moved by the empathy my team had shown their disconsolate teammate. As he had watched the scene unfold, he realized he wanted to develop that sense of camaraderie and community within his corporate team. He wondered if I would be interested in helping him do so. I said I would, in my spare time.

Polumbo was already good at executing business: strategies, planning, processes, and product delivery and service. What he wanted to work on was the people aspect of business. He needed instruction on how to dance between empathy and authority.

I helped Polumbo and his team learn to have more trust and understanding for each other, and that was the beginning of my journey into corporate team building and performance coaching. In the years since (I do it full-time now), I have identified seven steps of performance coaching. They are:

ENCOURAGE: Give power, strength, and confidence; supply belief; help release fear and doubt.

SUPPORT: Be present and available; participate and assist; reinforce and comfort.

CHALLENGE: Invite reflection, growth, and change; question everything and anything; demand honesty and clarity.

ENVISION: Dream and imagine; be intuitive; understand goals, plans, and process.

INSPIRE: Be a source of energy; give optimism, desire, and will; generate enthusiasm.

COUNSEL: Be an active listener—ask essential questions; understand ideas and feelings; care deeply and take a personal interest.

CENTER: Help focus and remember; offer calm performance confidence; celebrate, evaluate, and re-create.

As for the results to be derived from coaching, a portfolio manager for high-wealth individuals recently outlined the benefits his firm had received from a year of coaching: "The gift is that we all have a voice; a common language to express our feelings, desires, and frustrations. This voice translated across the firm, enabling previously smothered thoughts to be aired; encouraged understanding; and focused our attention on what were the primary roadblocks to our success. The benefit to all of us has been empowerment. We all realize we are where we are by choice. And in making that choice, we choose to be better teammates and encourage each other to succeed. My firm has gone from being great but lacking cohesion to incredible and united."

As for me, I especially thank John Polumbo for his encouragement and for giving me the opportunity to work with him and his team in the business world. I wonder where I would be today if my player had made the winning layup that night twelve years ago.

Walk Like a Champ

WHAT DOES EVERY CHAMPION POSSESS?

Passion and presence.

It is about that original drive; that love and desire to express ourselves and achieve something special that is impossible to attain without a level of internal motivation that comes from one place: a person's core.

"Champions aren't made in gyms," Muhammad Ali once remarked. "Champions are made from something they have deep inside them: a desire, a dream, a vision. They have to have late-minute stamina, they have to be a little faster, they have to have the skill and the will. But the will must be stronger than the skill."

Encouraging and supporting our own unique gifts, and understanding the power that resides within us, are paramount. We do that by staying positive and seeing the good in others, then praising them for it. They will return the favor many times over.

We wipe away those things that blur our positive attitude, not allowing our vision of the future to be obscured by negative thoughts—ours or anyone else's. We avoid telling ourselves negative things. There is enough negative energy assaulting us from all sides. Why let it come from within?

We associate with upstanding peers who aspire to be successful, and we set high standards and lofty goals. We look at problems as challenges and label them as such.

We engage in the process of identifying qualities necessary to reach our ultimate goal, and we incorporate in our daily lives those skills and attitudes that peak performers possess.

We take a personal inventory to strengthen our levels of confidence, courage, determination, compassion, perseverance, and leadership. We more fully discover what it is we really stand for, what we have to offer, and what we can be relied upon to give.

We create our own unique plan of action and begin to execute it. In the process, we become our own hero. We call the shots and set our own standard for excellence. We speak a language to ourselves and others that is uplifting, positive, and encouraging.

Our performance presence is the sum total of our beliefs, attitudes, experiences, and personal energies. When we are empowered and fired up, there is a purpose to our physical movement. People can see we are to be reckoned with and counted on. Our expression is one of relaxed self-confidence. We are not hurried, distracted, or swayed from our purpose. Each step and every accomplishment reinforce our place in the world.

We act with our goals in mind, envisioning great things. At times we surprise ourselves with a clarity we didn't know we possessed.

No matter how hard we work, there are no guarantees that we will win at everything we set out to accomplish. In truth, our personal victory depends on how we judge our own effort, rather than the official results, the score, the judges, our competitors, or other people's expectations.

Sure, we all want to win—first place, the medal, the prize—but winning first place does not necessarily mean winning the treasure.

The true treasure—the *real* victory—is when we apply our hardest effort, our best attitude, and our love for what we are doing.

With this attitude, we develop self-respect and self-confidence and become a true winner, possessing a treasure that no one can ever take from us.

That is our real victory.

PRACTICE: Pick an area in your life in which you are confident, such as: "I am a great dad." Take a walk, feeling and thinking that confidence. Feel your shoulders straighten, your breathing become calmer, and your pace get slower and more relaxed.

Then pick an area in which you are not so confident—such as earning enough money to support your family. Now, think about doing just that, and being financially successful. Feel it. Own it. Walk as if you are already wealthy. The first step to achieving a goal is to walk as if it has already happened.

Montana

I have noticed that a lot of professional athletes walk as if they are not in a hurry. They walk as if to say, "Here I am." I think it has to do with presence, confidence, and spending most of their time living in the moment.

How you feel about yourself plays a major role in how well you do. If you think you are beaten, you are. If you would like to win but think you can't, it's almost a cinch you won't. If you think you'll lose, you've already lost.

In sports or business, success begins with a person's state of mind and heart. Think big and your deeds will grow; think small and you'll fail. Think that you can, and you will. If you think you're outclassed, you are.

Life's victories don't always go to the strongest or smartest. Often the people who win are the ones who think they can and project that confidence.

One of my earliest dreams in life was to go to Notre Dame and play football for the legendary Ara Parseghian. Before I had a chance to play for Parseghian, he retired, and I found myself the number seven quarterback on the depth chart—meaning there were six guys who the coaches thought were better.

Up until that moment, I had always pictured myself in the starting lineup, and always on top. Those first couple of years at Notre Dame weren't easy; I had to fight my way up that depth chart. The coaches eventually gave me a shot and hung in with me through some tough times before we became national champions.

Looking back, I'm sure the only way I was able to become a starter—and eventually, an NFL draft selection—was by refusing to see myself as anything other than a winner. I believed it heart and soul, feeling that as long as I worked hard to prove myself and didn't give up, everything would work out.

Winners, I am convinced, imagine their dream first.

They want it with all their heart and expect it to come true.

There is, I believe, no other way to live.

Mitchell

During the early stages of our company, Joe wanted the three of us—including our other partner, Hilleary Hoskinson—to meet with his attorneys, Rob Mezzetti, Sr. and Jr. The father is an old-school Italian-American, known for his pugnacious character. Within the first five minutes of our meeting, he poked fun at Hilleary and me, yelled at us several times to speak louder, and demanded to know our true intentions. Nobody was going to try to take advantage of his client—whom he kept referring to as "The Champ"—on his watch. Fortunately, Mezzetti Sr. seemed to like us and, in the end, he thought our business concept a solid one.

What a cool name to be called—"The Champ." Although none of us is likely to be a four-time Super Bowl champion and a three-time MVP, we all would love to experience the feeling of being a champion. What does that mean? Do we have to win it all? Make the most sales? Earn the most money? Be the best in anything we do? Do we have to win the championship to possess the spirit of a champion?

If we are dependent upon the world's definition of a champion, then yes, we do need to win it all. We need to win the Super Bowl or the World Series, or dominate our chosen field and be the best, which means being better than everyone else.

However, that definition of being a champion is not entirely satisfying to me. The rest of us, I believe, need to internalize for ourselves this idea of being a champion. What does that mean in our own life? Although other people won't wear our name on the back of their shirt at the mall, how can we walk in the world with similar confidence and pride?

Walking like a champ means moving with the presence and the attitude that you make a difference. You walk and talk and work, knowing that what you do matters. Your life is not just about achieving success but about having a purpose and creating significance.

We want to show up every day with energy and enthusiasm. We want to bring not only our mind but our heart to our job, our work, our family, our friends, our community. We want to believe and know that a championship life lies ahead for us because a championship spirit lives inside of us.

Former boxing great Sugar Ray Leonard told me this story illustrating the importance of holding on to a championship mentality. Leonard was sitting in the stands at his first Wimbledon when he was approached by a tournament official. The official asked if Leonard would be willing to go into the locker room of one of the tennis players scheduled for the championship match. It seemed this particular player—the defending champion and one of the greatest female tennis players of all time—was unwilling to come out and begin the match. The official wondered if Leonard could speak to her and encourage her to come out. Leonard said, "No way. I don't even know her." Sometime later, the official came back and repeated the request. By then the entire crowd was getting anxious about the delayed match. Leonard agreed and entered the player's private locker room. "Who are you today?" asked Leonard. The player, filled with emotion, took a deep breath and said with resolve: "I'm the champion, that's who." Leonard nodded. "Good. I'm at the right place, then," he said, then went back to the stands. The player came out a few minutes later and went on to successfully defend her championship. After the match, the player sought out Leonard and thanked him for having the courage to challenge her and remind her of who she was. "We all lose it from time to time," Leonard explained to me. "We can get scared, have a panic attack, and forget who we are. It's good to have people around us who, from time to time, can help us remember about the champion within us."

If you ever find yourself losing touch with the champion spirit that resides within, remind yourself of the following:

It doesn't matter if you're not the best right now. Use your desire to improve. Have a burn inside. Want to get better.

Don't worry if other people don't believe in you. It doesn't matter. Believe in yourself. Know your strengths. Know your weaknesses. Get clear on the direction you want to go. Find what you love most about life. Show it as often as you possibly can.

Keep an open mind. Don't ever let someone ask how old you were when you realized that you knew everything. Ask questions, learn, and be humble, knowing there is always someone better, stronger, wiser.

Take your mental powers seriously. Learn to focus and concentrate. Activate your imagination. See your goals before you. Visualization takes practice, but it is worth it.

Walk like a champ. This statement is not symbolic or hopeful. To walk like a champion, you must think like a champion. You must feel like a champion. You must search, dig, fight, explore, ask, succeed, and fail, until you know beyond a doubt that the winning spirit lives inside you.

Take that walk.

Appreciate

IN THE MIDST OF STRIVING FOR EXCELLENCE, WE WANT TO TAKE CARE not to become so preoccupied with our goals and strategies that we neglect to develop a healthy spirit of appreciation for all that is good and right in our lives. Developing an attitude of gratitude is key to a happy and successful life. Too often in today's fast-paced, highly competitive world, we focus on fighting to get ahead at the cost of our health, family, and friends.

An attitude of appreciation can lead us in many directions, since there are boundless things for which to be grateful. The human body itself is an incomprehensible miracle, all the systems working in harmony. The heart beating in rhythm, digestion, respiration, circulation are all demonstrations of wondrous and superb team-work. Our skeletal and muscular systems, giving us the structure and freedom to move; the gifts of sight, sound, smell, taste, and touch. The power within our brain to think, communicate, and create. And, of course, the people in our lives; our ability to give and receive love. Our homes, our jobs, our health.

How can we experience the deep and profound impact that comes when we live in a state of appreciation? Developing an appreciative spirit takes work and a willingness to see what is good in life. We often look at what we don't have, focusing on what is missing. It's not easy for everyone to appreciate health or wealth. If someone is sick or poor or both, it may be difficult to see any hope or good. If we spend too much time in an office, out of touch with fresh air and natural beauty, it may be difficult to regularly appreciate the wonders of the outdoors. If someone is alone without family or many friends, it is difficult to be thankful for others. Regardless of our situation, a spirit of appreciation is an essential antidote for depression, cynicism, and negativity. It can be easily practiced, and the rewards are immense.

Appreciation should start at home and follow us throughout the day. When we integrate a spirit of gratitude into our daily lives, and honestly appreciate other people by acknowledging and thanking them, an experience of prosperity and abundance rapidly grows within us. We understand that the more thankful we are for what we have, and the more appreciation we give, the more we receive back.

Also, when we take time to appreciate, we find ourselves living more fully in the present moment. We are not only thinking about future plans or goals but experiencing present accomplishments as well. Appreciation leads to an engagement in the here and now.

As we explore the practice of appreciation, we not only acknowledge the gifts, talents, accomplishments, and other good fortune that has come our way; we also learn to appreciate the challenges, limitations, and obstacles we face. We let them motivate us to overcome our weaknesses and achieve even more in life.

PRACTICE: Who in your world deserves an outpouring of appreciation? Take a moment to identify three people, making a note of what it is you wish to convey to each one. What have they stood for in your life? How does their presence in your life affect you? Is there anything you would like them to know about how you have been impacted by their influence? Take time during the week to visit, write, call, or e-mail each one and thank them for their positive contributions to your life.

Montana

I am grateful for so much in life. I have always tried to tell and show those around me how much I appreciate them.

My appreciation starts, of course, with Mom and Dad.

My father, Joe Sr., was always ready to play catch with me and encourage my love of sports. It didn't escape my attention that the fathers of some other boys were too busy to play with their sons. My father always made me feel as if there was nothing he would rather be doing. I have tried to pass that on to my children. It may be the greatest lesson my father taught me.

I appreciate my mother, Theresa, for never wavering in her feelings toward me, whether I was in high school or enjoying success in football. She was always there to provide unconditional love and nurturing support (and help with my homework). When I'd come home with a bunch of friends in tow from playing sports, she knew how to stretch dinner for everyone and never complained about the extra mouths to feed. She helped ground me, and she taught me to appreciate the most important things in life: love and family. She passed away in 2004, and I miss her dearly.

I could not have done what I've done in sports, business, or life without my wife, Jennifer. She took the brunt of my erratic schedule during my playing days and gave me the space and time I needed to study. Jen maintained the care of our children and our home while pursuing her own successful career as a model and TV spokesperson. She gave me a wonderful family to come home to every day. She helped boost my level of confidence and provided me with emotional support when things got difficult. When I was on the road and missing the family, she would overnight me new pictures she had taken, with funny handwritten captions—like one of the girls standing with her arms in the air, saying: "Throw one for me, Daddy."

One Super Bowl year, the two weeks before the game were particularly brutal. The pressure from the media was building, and we also had a houseful of extended family and visitors in town for the game. I was ready to lose my mind, and at one point, in frustration, I nearly smashed a mirrored closet door. Jennifer took over, quietly and efficiently. "We're going to check you in to the hotel," she said, and she started packing my bag. "Go wait in the car." She took me to the hotel so I could find some peace and quiet to study my playbook. In little and big ways, Jen has always been there for me. I appreciate her every single day of my life. I'm a lucky man.

My children, daughters Alexandra and Elizabeth and sons Nathaniel and Nicholas, have been my leveling factor. They don't care what I did in the past or what others think of me. I'm just Dad, and when I come home, it's time to wrestle or shoot baskets or go play in the pool. They just want me to be dedicated to them, which is the easiest thing for me to do. As they grow older—our two girls are now in college—I miss those days of youth and innocence, when Jennifer and I could protect them. Now we're having to let them go out a little more on their own, and see how they handle the world.

I have so much appreciation for all my hardworking teammates over the years, from my high school days, through college, right into the pros. With football being such a team sport, I would not have achieved what I did without their efforts. The same goes for all my coaches, who taught me so much.

I am appreciative of the fans, too. Yes, I know they didn't hesitate to boo me at times, but that was their right. Deep down, I feel that I established a tremendous relationship with the people of San Francisco and football fans across the country. It meant a lot to me as a player.

One man who was there for me from the beginning of my career has a special place in my heart: Eddie DeBartolo, Jr., the former owner of the 49ers. Eddie has been there from the day I was drafted right up until today, a supportive and giving friend not just to me but to my entire family. "Mr. D.," as I called him when I was lucky enough to play for his team, in so many ways set the tone for the 49ers as world champions—not only with his own winning spirit but also in the way he treated us like winners from the beginning, before we actually were. He is one of a kind, and I am lucky to call him my friend.

Whether it's family, friends, or colleagues, we should never fail to let the most important people in our lives know how much we appreciate them, and how much credit we share with them for whatever success we've attained.

Mitchell

Last year I was talking with top leaders of the McDonald's Corporation on the subject of integrating and applying appreciation within their corporate team. The session was scheduled to last one hour. I told the group we were going to do an exercise to "profoundly acknowledge and appreciate" their impact on the team. I described this as a principle of success and said, "If you just slightly improve in this area, your team will work much better together." The ground rules I set up allowed for no negative comments. It wasn't a time for fixing anything or voicing complaints. The goal was to acknowledge an individual or the entire team for something specific that had made an enormous difference in their lives in the past year.

Once they started acknowledging and appreciating, the group members became so engaged with the exercise that we were still at it three hours later. I was impressed with how much togetherness, camaraderie, and team spirit they were developing and how willing they seemed to appreciate one another.

The spirit of appreciation comes in all forms. Living in the heart of wine country in Northern California allows me to spend time with a lot of people in the wine industry. When talking with Armando Ceja at his small, family-owned Napa vineyard, one cannot escape an almost overpowering sense of appreciation that he has for the land. Taking nothing for granted, Armando works with, and connects to, all the elements that result in his award-winning wines. When he works in the vineyards—pruning, tilling the soil, or harvesting the fruit—one can almost see the connection between the man, his wine, and the land. This appreciative spirit has accompanied Armando and his family as they have evolved from farmworkers to vineyard owners and, ultimately, to premium winemakers.

As for my own appreciation, I would be remiss not mentioning some people who have given me their love and friendship and have made the biggest impact during my journey of learning and teaching.

Bill and Marie Mitchell, my father and mother, have been and continue to be a consistent source of support and encouragement. What I most appreciate about my parents is how much time they devoted to our family. Growing up, they created such a warm feeling in our home that my friends always wanted to hang out at our house. I grew up knowing that I was loved.

Bill and Doug, my older brothers, taught me how to compete. They let me know that they would protect me, no matter the situation. With them around, I always felt safe, knowing they had my best interests at heart. They gave me the true experience of brotherhood.

Adele, my wife of twenty-five years, has always seen in me the person I truly am, even when I couldn't see it myself. After graduating from college, I had not a clue as to what career path I wanted to pursue. Adele saw me as a success regardless of what path I chose. She told me over and over again that I could do whatever I set my mind on and whatever I put my heart into. It is a real gift when someone truly believes in you that much.

Adele and I were married almost ten years before our first child was born. We felt sad that having children might not happen for us, though Adele never gave up hope. One day when I was coaching my team, Adele walked into the gym. I was worried when I saw her because she never came to practice. She walked up to me with a smile and told me she was pregnant. Joyful tears rolled down my cheeks. After she left, my players lifted me up and carried me around the gym, celebrating my impending fatherhood. I believe that Adele's attitude—her belief, hope, and optimism—was strong enough to overcome whatever the natural odds were against our having children.

Carmen and Antonia, our daughters, have been the inspiration behind so much of what I do. Their passion and enthusiasm for life have helped me stay focused on what is most important. I am thankful and honored to be their father.

Chris Mullin, five-time all-star NBA player, has played an amazing role in my life and had a huge impact. His invitation for me to work side by side with him in the NBA over the past ten years has been a dream come true. I appreciate his openheartedness, as well as his tough-mindedness.

While Mully opened the door for me, it was Chris Cohan, owner of the Golden State Warriors, who invited me in. Over the years, he has taught me valuable lessons, and I want to express my gratitude for his giving me the opportunity to work with him and his organization.

Lani Dy, my real estate partner, is a person who understands how to turn dreams into reality. I appreciate her off-the-charts energy and determination. She has inspired my entire family by sharing with us her own principles of success.

Lastly, I want to express my appreciation of Joe Montana, a man with awe-inspiring status and down-to-earth approachability.

With a willingness to play big no matter what the game, Joe has achieved a level of success not matched by many. I respect his collaborative spirit and his commitment to sharing his experience and knowledge of winning with others. Joe carries with him wherever he goes the torch of the winning spirit.

Acknowledgments

WE HAD A GREAT TEAM SUPPORTING US IN THE CREATION OF THIS BOOK.

Hilleary Hoskinson was an inspiration. Long before anyone else, he believed in this book, our company, and all that will follow.

Writer Bruce Henderson helped us turn our thoughts and ideas into the written word and expertly guided us through the entire editorial process.

Literary agent Paul Bresnick served as our able advocate in the publishing industry and helped us find the right publisher, Random House.

Senior editor Caroline Sutton was the right editor, too. She gave us her innovative ideas, enthusiasm, and unqualified support at every turn.

We thank the many individuals from the worlds of sports, business, and personal development who contributed stories, reminiscences, and ideas. They include: Carol Adams, Emil Bohn, Brian Boitano, Matt Byrd, John Cashman, Tony Daloisio, Charles Darr, John DiBenedetto, Dissero Partners, George Dy, Mark Grabow, Teresa Hargrave, Phil Jackson, Roshi Kwong, Sugar Ray Leonard, Ronnie Lott, Choeleen Loundagin, Maxcomm Inc., Jim McCarthy, Joe Milam, Tony Milner, Kimchi Moyer, Chris Mullin, George Mumford, Kim Navarro, Dennis Park, John Polumbo, Robert Rowell, Irena Schwaderer, John Springer, Cynthia Stringer, Mel Suhd, Dave Toole, Bill Walsh, and John Wooden.

About the Authors

JOE MONTANA led the San Francisco 49ers to four Super Bowl victories and is the only three-time Super Bowl MVP. Drafted in the third round in 1979, Montana was inducted into the Pro Football Hall of Fame in 2000. Since retiring from professional football, he has become a popular motivational speaker and co-founder of MVP Performance Institute (www.MVPperformance.com), a consulting company that trains business executives and others in improving individual and organizational performance. He lives in Northern California.

TOM MITCHELL, PH.D., is a business coach, motivational speaker, and performance consultant. A former college head basketball coach, he advises the NBA as well as major corporations. Along with Joe Montana, he founded the MVP Performance Institute to bring their proven skills to a wider audience. He lives in Santa Rosa, California.

About the Type

This book was set in Bembo, a typeface based on an old-style Roman face that was used for Cardinal Bembo's tract *De Aetna* in 1495. Bembo was cut by Francisco Griffo in the early sixteenth century. The Lanston Monotype Machine Company of Philadelphia brought the well-proportioned letter forms of Bembo to the United States in the 1930s.